THE HAIRY BIKERS'

ASIAN ADVENTURE

SI KING & DAVE MYERS

THE HAIRY BIKERS'
ASIAN ADVENTURE

SI KING & DAVE MYERS

WEIDENFELD & NICOLSON

Cookbooks are a collaborative effort so we'd like to dedicate this one to our great team. Everyone has worked their socks off to help us put this beautiful book together and we are very, very proud of it.

Dave and Si

CONTENTS

OUR ASIAN ADVENTURE

We're lucky lads. We've been off on our travels again – this time to Asia to discover all kinds of wonderful things to eat and cook. And what a time we've had. This trip has been our dream for years and it certainly didn't disappoint. Asian food is fresh, tasty and exciting, with so many different textures and lively flavour combinations. We love it more than ever now and we'd like to share our favourite dishes with you.

Asian food is so much more familiar now in Britain. Who would have thought a few years ago that you'd find sushi in service stations and sandwich bars? Ever since we started writing books and making programmes about food, we've wanted to make a trip to Asia. We were keen to find out about some of these great cuisines and learn authentic recipes and skills we could use at home. To be honest, the book we've come up with is one that we wanted for ourselves, something that will always be in our kitchens. It's our go-to manual for cooking the Asian food we love and we hope it will be yours too.

Our Asian adventure started in Hong Kong with Cantonese food – perhaps one of the most familiar to us in Britain. A visit to the local takeaway or Chinese restaurant is the first experience of Asian food for many of us – and who doesn't love sweet and sour pork! We went on to sample the culinary delights of Japan and Thailand and then to enjoy the bold, spicy food of Korea – less well known to us but oh so good.

RECIPES TO COOK AT HOME

You might think this kind of food is tricky to prepare but it's really not. The main ingredients are things you cook with all the time, like chicken, beef, pork, fish and prawns. Yes, there are few things in the recipes that you might not have heard of but we'll help you with those and soon you'll be a dab hand with the dashi. We've come back with a great range of recipes for you to cook at home; from simple family supper dishes to more fancy feasts for the ones you love. And don't think we've abandoned our quest for healthy eating. While some of these dishes are quite hearty, there are loads of recipes that are packed with flavour but not too high in calories. They fit our mantra of taste first, calories second, perfectly.

One of the wonderful things about many Asian dishes is that they're quick. Whack it all in a wok and you've supper on the table in no time. You do need to think ahead a bit and get everything in, and some dishes also need marinating, but it's not difficult. The important thing is to have everything chopped, grated, peeled and crushed before you start cooking, then the rest is a breeze. Chefs call this sort of preparation 'mise en place'; we call it getting all your bits ready.

You don't need lots of special equipment. We visited a family in their apartment in Hong Kong where grandma cooked up a storm, producing a banquet for six with a wok and one gas ring. We barely saw an oven the whole time we were away. Certain techniques such as stir-frying are common throughout Asia so once you get the hang of these, you're flying.

DISCOVERIES

One thing that we hadn't realised was the amount of regional variation. Thailand, for example, is almost as big as France and has as much diversity in its cooking. The food in Tokyo is so different from the meals we had in the more traditional city of Kyoto. But the big discovery was street food. It's everywhere and we ate anything we could get our hands on. People pick up onigiri rice balls, for example, for a quick bite just like we might grab a pasty at the garage. In the market in Tokyo everyone was eating octopus balls when we might dig into a bag of chips. Eating out in some of these countries is so good and so cheap that it's a way of life for many people. In Bangkok there are apartments built without kitchens because people don't need or use them!

An Asian meal doesn't necessarily follow the same structure as ours – starter, main and pud – and a number of dishes may be served together at a meal and all have equal importance. By all means, create your own banquets if you fancy but it's fine just to pick and mix the recipes you like and serve them up to your family in the regular way. How about trying a green papaya salad followed by some prawn katsu burgers, then something from our puds chapter?

Now – puddings. We did struggle to find desserts that suited our western palates, particularly in terms of texture. We've included a couple of proper Asian cakes and puddings but we've also come up with our own ideas, using local ingredients such as papaya and coconut. We love them so we hope you do too.

Our Asian adventure was a mind-blowing experience and we learned so much about the food of the countries we visited. We discovered some amazing dishes and we came back more excited than ever about Asian food. So get ready to tantalise your taste buds and get cooking Asian-style.

ROCK YOUR WOK

You can do almost anything with a wok – stir-fry, pan fry, braise, steam, smoke food, protect yourself from the rain! You can use a frying pan of course but woks are available everywhere from kitchen shops to supermarkets and you can get one for around a tenner.

A traditional wok is made of carbon steel. Before you use your wok for the first time, you need to wash and season it. To do this, scrub the wok well, then rinse and put it on a low heat to dry thoroughly. When it's dry, pour in a couple of tablespoons of groundnut or vegetable oil and heat gently. Carefully wipe the warm oil over the inside of the wok with some kitchen paper. Continue to heat for 10 minutes or so, wiping the oil over the surface of the wok occasionally. The wok will start to darken in colour, which means it is now seasoned.

Once you've done this, clean your wok gently after use and don't scour unless you have to. If you do need to scrub off any burnt food or rust from your wok, season again after cleaning.

KNOW YOUR INGREDIENTS

Some of the recipes do have long lists of ingredients, but don't worry – you'll find that many of them are spices and seasonings that are added in a flash. You might spot some that are unfamiliar to you but we've put together a little guide, which you'll find on pages 298—305. This will tell you all you need to know in order to cook the recipes in this book.

The big supermarkets all stock plenty of Asian ingredients but we've also included a list of specialist shops and online suppliers (see pages 306–308). Once you have your basics you're away. We find it useful to keep all our Asian spices, sauces and flavourings together in a box so it's all handy when you want to cook something.

Obviously the more of the proper stuff you can get the more authentic your recipe will taste, but don't panic if you can't find everything and you have to use ordinary shallots instead of Thai or regular basil instead of holy basil. The dish might not taste quite how it does in Chiang Mai but it will still be good.

HAVE YOU HAD YOUR RICE YET?

Rice is the cornerstone of Asian food. It's so important that the morning greeting in Hong Kong is 'Have you had your rice yet?'. When we were filming our Asian Adventure we spent a day in a paddy field in Thailand. We couldn't believe what hard work it was and we'll never take a grain of rice for granted again.

We use four main types in this book.
*   Long-grain – the rice that's usually served with Hong Kong Cantonese cooking.
*   Jasmine or fragrant rice, which is lovely with Thai meals.
*   Japanese rice, which is short-grain and quite sticky when cooked. It's sometimes labelled sushi rice in this country.
*   Glutinous rice, which is extra sticky for use in certain recipes.

For all these kinds of rice, follow the cooking instructions on the packet.

A FEW LITTLE NOTES FROM US

Weigh your ingredients carefully and use proper teaspoons and tablespoons and a measuring jug. With spices, the difference between half a teaspoon and a teaspoon can affect the taste and flavour balance of a recipe.

All root ginger, onions, garlic and shallots should be peeled, unless otherwise specified.

We've judged the amount of fresh chilli in a recipe as carefully as we can, but chillies do vary in hotness so keep tasting. You can always add more heat but you can't take it out!

We've made cooking times as accurate as we can, but always check that your food is properly cooked.

HONG KONG

Ultra-modern yet deeply traditional, Hong Kong is the place where the past meets the present, where East meets West. This extraordinary city is the gateway to China and just the place for two Brits to start a culinary adventure. And what an adventure it was. We made fresh dim sum in one of the most famous dim sum places in a Hong Kong market – and found it almost impossible not to eat more than we made! We went dragon boat racing. We cooked on a dai pan dong – a kind of street food stall – and served up our dish to Alvin Leung, a local Michelin-starred chef.

Best of all in Hong Kong, though, was the home cooking. We were lucky enough to be invited to share supper at the home of Grandma Lulu who, with just a wok and a chopper, cooked up a banquet for six in her family's little apartment. It was real local food – comforting, tasty and full of flavour. You'll find her recipe for sweet and sour pork in this chapter so give it a try and you'll see what we mean.

We ate everything we could get our hands on and we feasted our eyes on yet more delights, including ingredients we'd never seen or heard of before. But just to reassure you, the recipes we've brought back contain familiar favourites such as prawns, chicken, beef and fish, plus some special seasonings and sauces, and they're perfectly possible to make in your kitchen at home. No chicken feet or snake soup, we promise; just some sizzlingly good food!

CHOW MEIN

Everyone knows this one and so here's our version of the classic – dead good, though we say it ourselves. If you'd like a crunchy noodle topping, fry some extra rice noodles before you begin to make the chow mein. Alternatively, top with a handful of ready-made prawn or shrimp crackers.

Place the pork fillet on a chopping board and, using a sharp knife, carefully trim off as much excess fat and sinew as you can. Cut the pork in half lengthways and then cut it into thin slices. Put the pork slices in a bowl and toss them with the five-spice powder, salt and plenty of black pepper. Set aside.

Half fill a medium pan with water and bring it to the boil. Add the egg noodles and swish them around in the hot water with a long wooden spoon to separate the strands. Return to the boil and cook for 3–4 minutes, or according to the packet instructions, until tender. Drain the noodles, then rinse them in a sieve under running water until cold. Toss with a tablespoon of the oil and set aside.

Mix the sugar and cornflour together in a bowl and gradually stir in the soy sauce, mirin and 100ml of water. Set aside.

Heat a tablespoon of oil in a large non-stick frying pan or a wok. Stir-fry the pork over a high heat for 2 minutes or until nicely browned. Tip the pork on to a plate and put the pan back on the heat.

Add another tablespoon of the oil and stir-fry the red pepper and carrot for 2 minutes. Add the ginger, garlic, spring onions, peas and water chestnuts and stir-fry together for 2 minutes more until softened but not soggy. Tip everything on to a plate.

Pour the remaining oil into the pan and add the noodles. Stir-fry the noodles for 2–3 minutes, or until they are beginning to become lovely and crispy and golden-brown. Return the meat and vegetables to the pan and stir-fry together, tossing all the ingredients with 2 long-handled spoons for 1–2 minutes, or until evenly mixed and piping hot.

Stir the soy mixture to combine the ingredients again and pour it into the pan. Continue tossing everything together for another couple of minutes, or until hot and glossy. Serve immediately, topped with more fried noodles or prawn crackers.

Serves 4

500g pork fillet (tenderloin)
1 tsp Chinese five-spice powder
½ tsp flaked sea salt
200g dried medium egg noodles
4 tbsp vegetable or groundnut oil
2 tbsp soft light brown sugar
2 tsp cornflour
4 tbsp dark soy sauce
2 tbsp mirin
1 red pepper, deseeded and sliced
1 large carrot, peeled and cut into
    matchsticks about 6cm long
25g fresh root ginger, peeled
    and very finely sliced
3 garlic cloves, very finely sliced
6 spring onions, trimmed
    and sliced
50g frozen peas
225g canned water chestnuts,
    drained and halved
extra handful of fried noodles or
    prawn crackers, for serving
freshly ground black pepper

CHINESE BEEF CURRY

Chinese curries have a unique character which we're familiar with from takeaways. This is the sort of dish we grew to love as kids, but now we make it ourselves. It's not that hot, but you can pep it up if you like by using extra chilli powder. The flavours are classic Asian – anise, orange and soy sauce – and they're delicious.

Pour half the oil into a large, heavy-based pan and place it over a high heat. Season the meat with a generous amount of salt and pepper and once the oil is smoking hot, add the meat and brown it all over. This will take a few minutes and you will probably need to brown the meat in a few batches so you don't overcrowd the pan. Remove each batch from the pan and place it on a plate while you brown the rest.

Reduce the heat to medium and add the remaining oil. Add the onions and red peppers and allow them to sweat for a few minutes until they are just beginning to soften. Add the ginger and garlic and continue to cook for a further minute before adding the star anise, cinnamon stick, orange peel, curry powder and chilli powder. Sprinkle in the cornflour and fry the whole mixture for a further minute, stirring regularly to stop the spices from burning. There should be a gorgeous smell coming from your pan now.

Tip the browned meat, along with any juices that have gathered, back into the pan and stir to mix all the ingredients together. Turn up the heat to maximum, and once sizzling pour in the Shaoxing wine. Let it bubble away until the liquid is reduced by about half, then pour in the stock, and bring the whole lot to the boil. Skim any scum that rises to the top before reducing the heat to a simmer.

Put the lid on the pan, placing it slightly askew so the pan isn't quite covered, and leave the curry to simmer. Keep an eye on it, as you may need to add a little more liquid to stop your curry from sticking on the bottom of the pan. After about an hour, test the meat – you want meltingly tender chunks of beef. If it's not tender enough, continue to simmer for a total of up to 2–2 ½ hours.

When you are happy with the tenderness of your meat, stir in the soy sauce and chopped coriander (if using) and serve with bowls of rice.

Serves 4–6

4 tbsp groundnut or vegetable oil
1.25kg boneless beef shin, chopped into 3cm chunks
2 onions, roughly chopped
2 red peppers, deseeded and cut into 2cm chunks
30g fresh root ginger, peeled and finely sliced
4 garlic cloves, finely chopped
2 star anise
1 cinnamon stick, snapped in half
strip of orange peel, about 8 x 2cm
1 heaped tbsp curry powder
2 tsp chilli powder (more if you like)
1 tbsp cornflour
100ml Shaoxing rice wine
700ml beef stock
50ml soy sauce
chopped coriander, for serving (optional)
freshly cooked rice, for serving
flaked sea salt
freshly ground black pepper

CLASSY CRISPY BEEF AND BLACK BEANS

We're going for a drier than usual stir-fry here, which we think makes for a lovely fresh-tasting dish and a change from the wetter versions. It's topped with fresh cucumber – not traditional, but a nice touch – and makes a little beef go a long way. Super-moreish, we warn you.

Put the sliced steak into a bowl and add the Shaoxing wine, sugar and 1 tablespoon of the soy sauce. Add 1 of the finely chopped garlic cloves and mix well to combine. Leave the beef to marinate for at least an hour, but preferably overnight.

When you're ready to cook, prepare all the remaining ingredients. Pour oil into a wok or high-sided saucepan to a depth of about 7.5cm and heat the oil to about 180°C. Do not allow the oil to overheat and don't leave the pan unattended.

While the oil is heating, tip the beef into a sieve and try to remove as much excess liquid as possible. Place the cornflour in a bowl and season with salt and pepper, then add the drained beef slices and toss them around until they are coated with the cornflour. The meat and cornflour might clag up a bit at this point. Don't worry too much, but try to separate the meat into individual strips before frying.

You'll need to cook the beef in batches so you don't overcrowd the pan. Carefully drop some strips of beef into the hot oil and cook for about 2 minutes, by which time the strips should be crispy and look rather like Twiglets. Remove the beef with a slotted spoon and leave to drain on kitchen paper while you fry the rest.

When all the beef is cooked, heat the 2 tablespoons of oil in a clean wok over a medium to high heat. When the oil is hot, add the diced onion, the carrot and red pepper, and stir-fry for 1 minute until the vegetables are just beginning to soften. Rinse the black beans under a cold tap to remove any excess salt, then add them to the pan with the rest of the garlic and continue to stir-fry for a further minute.

Add the crispy beef to the vegetables and beans and toss to incorporate. Serve topped with fresh cucumber and coriander and basil leaves.

Serves 2 as a main course with rice, or 4 as part of a larger meal

300g rump steak, sliced into strips about 50mm thick and 4cm long
2 tbsp Shaoxing rice wine
2 tsp sugar
3 tbsp soy sauce
3 garlic cloves, finely chopped
groundnut or vegetable oil, for deep-frying, plus 2 tbsp
3 tbsp cornflour
1 small red onion, roughly diced
1 small carrot, peeled and sliced into half moons about the thickness of pound coins
½ red pepper, deseeded and chopped into 2cm chunks
2 tbsp fermented black beans
½ cucumber, deseeded and chopped into pieces about the same size as the beef
small bunch each of fresh coriander and basil leaves, leaves picked from the stems, for serving
flaked sea salt
freshly ground black pepper

FIVE-SPICE BELLY PORK

One of our favourites. Everyone loves belly pork and we couldn't go to Hong Kong and not come back with a recipe. This one is just about perfect, we reckon.

Crush the peppercorns and star anise in a pestle and mortar or a spice grinder, then tip them into a large plastic food bag. You need something that's big enough to hold the pork and has a top you can seal, such as a zip and seal plastic bag.

Add the remaining ingredients, including the pork, to the bag, then massage the mixture into the meat through the bag. Seal the top of the bag and leave the pork to marinate for 24 hours or longer in the fridge. The longer the meat is marinated the more flavour there will be.

When you're ready to cook the pork, preheat the oven to 150°C/Fan 130°C/Gas 2. Place the pork in a roasting tin – it should fit tightly – with the marinade and add 50ml of water to the tin. Roast the pork for 2 ½ hours or until the meat is tender and crispy. Check every now and then to make sure it's not drying out and add a little more water if necessary. Turn up the heat to 200°C/Fan 180°C/Gas 6 for the last 15 minutes to get the pork really crisp.

Serve with some pak choi drizzled with toasted sesame oil and freshly cooked rice. This pork is also good with the stir-fried tomatoes and eggs on page 48.

Serves 4

2 tsp Sichuan peppercorns

2 star anise

1kg belly pork, skin scored

2 tsp Chinese five-spice powder

4 garlic cloves, finely grated

30g fresh root ginger, peeled
    and finely grated

6 tbsp hoisin sauce

2 tbsp sesame oil

4 tbsp soy sauce

2 tsp grated palm sugar
    or caster sugar

1 tsp salt

KING PRAWN AND SCALLOP STIR-FRY

We cooked this dish in Hong Kong on a kind of a street restaurant stall called a dai pai dong. We were advised to thicken the sauce with cornflour so the wonderfully flavourful juices cling to the crisp veggies and fish, and this suggestion worked brilliantly. This is a quick cook so get all your ingredients ready before you start and you'll have a treat in no time.

Place a wok on the hob and heat until it is smoking, then add the groundnut oil. When the oil is hot, add the garlic and ginger and cook them for 1 minute until soft. Keep stirring.

Add the prawns to the garlic and ginger and stir-fry for 1 minute. Toss the wok frequently or keep the prawns moving with a spatula.

Season the scallops with salt and pepper and lay them around the edge of the hot wok so they get a little colour on their sides.

Toss the wok again or gently turn the seafood over, then add the rice wine. Add the prepared greens, mangetout and spring onion, then gently toss for a couple of minutes until all the vegetables have wilted slightly. Add the red chilli, soy sauce and the cornflour and water mixture and keep on the heat for another minute until the cornflour is cooked and the sauce has thickened.

Divide the mixture between 2 bowls and sprinkle ½ a teaspoon of sesame oil over each portion. Serve at once!

Serves 2

2 tbsp groundnut oil

1 garlic clove, thinly sliced

10g fresh root ginger, cut into matchsticks

6 raw king prawns, peeled and deveined

3 scallops, cut in half to make 6 discs

1 ½ tbsp Shaoxing rice wine

4 sprigs of choi sum (Chinese broccoli)

1 pak choi, cut into 4

30g mangetout, each cut in half lengthways at an angle

1 spring onion, cut into 3 and then into strips

½ red chilli, thinly sliced at a jaunty angle

2 tbsp light soy sauce

1 tbsp cornflour, mixed with 2 tbsp cold water

1 tsp sesame oil

flaked sea salt

freshly ground black pepper

PORK AND PRAWN DIM SUM

These little parcels of deliciousness are becoming more and more popular in the UK. We travelled to Hong Kong to feast on some of the best and we've also picked up some top tips to share with you. By the way, something we learned is that toasted sesame oil is for dressing and finishing a dish only, not for cooking.

In a large bowl, mix together the prawns, pork, coriander, ginger, grated garlic, garlic roots or spring onions, sesame oil, rice vinegar, soy sauce, tablespoon of cornflour, peppercorns and salt. Get in there with your clean hands and mix well so that all the ingredients are thoroughly incorporated, then set aside for 2–3 hours for the flavours to develop.

When you're ready to make your dim sum, mix the remaining teaspoon of cornflour with 2 tablespoons of cold water for sealing the dim sum. Oil a stainless steel or bamboo steamer and line it with a banana leaf or baking parchment – it's important that the dim sum don't stick so prepare the steamer with care.

Take a wonton wrapper and brush around the edges with the cornflour and water mix. Make sure you brush well – don't stint on this. Place the wrapper on the palm of your hand and put a good teaspoon of the pork and prawn mixture in the centre of the wrapper, being careful not to overfill it.

Gradually and carefully fold the sides up around the filling. Cupping the dim sum between your thumb and forefinger, use a damp teaspoon to press the mixture and make a smooth top. Add a pea on top, then place the filled dim sum on the steamer and repeat until all the mixture is used up.

Place the steamer over a pan of boiling water and steam the dim sum for 15 minutes. Drizzle with toasted sesame oil and serve with a bowl of soy sauce for dipping.

Makes 18

150g raw, peeled king prawns, deveined and chopped
250g minced pork
50g fresh coriander (with root), chopped
35g fresh root ginger, finely grated
3 large garlic cloves, grated
2 fresh garlic roots or 3 spring onions, finely sliced
2 tbsp sesame oil
1 ½ tbsp rice vinegar
1 ½ tbsp dark soy sauce
1 tbsp cornflour, plus 1 tsp
1 tsp Sichuan peppercorns, crushed
1 tsp flaked sea salt, crushed
vegetable oil, for greasing
18 wonton wrappers
18 frozen peas, to garnish
toasted sesame oil, for drizzling
soy sauce, for dipping

PRAWN AND CRAB DIM SUM

Dim sum are so incredibly delicious that we find it hard ever to make enough. You can buy frozen dim sum but home-made are so much better – it's like comparing factory white sliced to a home-made loaf. These really are worth the effort and make a great little starter.

Put the chopped prawns and crabmeat in a large bowl and add the ginger and garlic. Drain and squeeze the orange peel, chop it finely, then add it to the bowl with the garlic chives (or spring onions), water chestnuts and diced carrot.

Add 2 teaspoons of the cornflour and a good pinch of salt and pepper, then mix well until the ingredients are thoroughly combined. Cover the bowl with cling film and place it in the fridge for 45 minutes for the flavours to develop and the mixture to firm up.

When you're ready to make your dim sum, mix the remaining teaspoon of cornflour with 2 tablespoons of cold water for sealing the dim sum. Oil a stainless steel or bamboo steamer and line it with a banana leaf or baking parchment – it's important that the dim sum don't stick, so prepare the steamer with care.

Take a wonton wrapper and brush around the edges with the cornflour and water mix. Make sure you brush well – don't stint on this. Place the wrapper on the palm of your hand and put a good teaspoon of the prawn and crab mixture in the centre of your wrapper, being careful not to overfill it.

Gradually and carefully fold the sides up around the filling. Cupping the dim sum between your thumb and forefinger, use a damp teaspoon to press the mixture and make a smooth top. Place the filled dim sum on the steamer and repeat until all the mixture is used up.

Place the steamer over a pan of boiling water and steam the dim sum for 15 minutes. Serve with soy sauce for dipping.

Makes 18

150g raw, peeled tiger prawns, deveined and chopped
100g fresh white crabmeat
15g fresh root ginger, finely grated
2 garlic cloves, finely grated
5g dried orange peel, soaked in boiling water for 20 minutes
6 garlic chives or 2 spring onions, finely sliced
3 canned water chestnuts, diced
1 small carrot, peeled and diced
3 tsp cornflour
vegetable oil, for greasing
18 wonton wrappers
soy sauce, for dipping
flaked sea salt
freshly ground black pepper

PORK WITH WIDE NOODLES
PORK HO FUN

The meat in this dish is 'velveted' which means it is marinated in a mixture that tenderises it naturally. The same method can be used with all meats. Ho fun noodles are wide and flat – a bit like a Chinese version of pappardelle. They work perfectly for this but ordinary egg noodles would be fine too.

Place the egg white, cornflour and soy sauce in a bowl. Use a small whisk or a fork to mix all the ingredients together until well combined. Tip the sliced meat into the mixture and stir it around so that all the pieces of meat are well coated. Leave the meat to marinate for at least 2 hours, but preferably 3–4 hours.

Bring a large pan of water to the boil. Add the broccoli, bring the water back to the boil and boil for 1 minute before removing it with a slotted spoon. Refresh the broccoli immediately under cold water.

Keep the water boiling while you carefully remove the egg white mixture from the pork pieces. You don't have to be too meticulous about this – just try to remove as much as you can without going mad. Drop the meat into the boiling water and cook for 1 minute before tipping it into a colander. Leave the meat to one side while you prepare the rest of the dish.

Now blanch the noodles by plunging them into a saucepan of boiling water. Leave for them 45 seconds to a minute only, then drain and set aside. Don't overcook the noodles or they will be sticky and gloopy.

Heat the groundnut oil in a wok or large pan over a high heat. Once it's hot, add the garlic, chillies, spring onions and dried shrimps. Stir-fry for a couple of minutes before adding the blanched pork and broccoli, then continue to stir-fry for a further minute. Add the blanched noodles to the pan, carefully separating them with your fingers, and add the soy sauce and oyster sauce.

Stir-fry everything together for a minute or so before serving.

Serves 4

1 egg white
2 tbsp cornflour
2 tbsp soy sauce
450g pork tenderloin, cut into
    slices 1cm thick
250g tenderstem broccoli, thick
    stalks split lengthways
2 tbsp groundnut oil
6 garlic cloves, finely chopped
2 red chillies, deseeded and finely
    sliced at an angle
4 spring onions, trimmed and
    sliced into 2cm pieces
2 tbsp dried shrimps
500g ho fun noodles
2 tbsp soy sauce
2 tbsp oyster sauce

EGG FRIED RICE

Egg fried rice is a great everyday tummy filler and the perfect way of using leftovers to make a comforting little supper that's lovely on its own or as a side dish. You can add all sorts of fillings but it is best made with rice that's been cooked and left to cool. Use some ham or bacon if you like instead of the belly pork.

Cook the rice according to the directions on the packet and leave to cool.

Whisk the eggs with the sesame oil and a good pinch of salt. Heat a non-stick frying pan or a wok with a drizzle of groundnut oil and when the oil is fairly hot, pour in the egg mixture. Do not stir and let the egg cook gently for a minute until the bottom starts to set. Then, using a rubber spatula, gently push one side of the egg mixture into the centre of the wok and tilt the wok to allow the still liquid egg to flow underneath and cook.

Slide the cooked omelette on to a plate and roll it up into a cigar shape. Cut it into 1cm slices, then cover with foil and set it aside to keep warm while you prepare the rice.

Heat 2 tablespoons of groundnut oil in the pan. Drain the dried shrimp and add them to the pan with the diced belly pork and garlic, then heat through for about 45 seconds.

Grind the peppercorns in a pestle and mortar and add them to the pan along with the Chinese five-spice. Then add the rice and stir-fry for 4–5 minutes, tossing everything together frequently to blend all the flavours.

Add the peeled prawns and spring onions, then check the seasoning, adding some freshly ground white pepper if necessary. Carefully fold in the strips of omelette, then serve at once with some soy sauce.

Serves 4

2 large eggs
1 tsp sesame oil
groundnut oil, for frying
60g small dried shrimp, soaked in hot water
100g cooked 5-spice belly pork (see p. 22), chopped into 1cm cubes
1 garlic clove, finely chopped
¾ tsp Sichuan peppercorns
1 tsp Chinese five-spice powder
120g rice
60g cooked peeled prawns, defrosted and drained
3 spring onions, sliced at an angle (including green parts)
soy sauce, for serving
flaked sea salt
freshly ground white pepper

LOTUS LEAF WRAPS
LO MAI GAI

We love this popular dim sum dish, which is made by steaming lotus leaves filled with sticky rice, Chinese sausages, chicken, pork and lots of vegetables. Yum yum, dim sum...

Start preparations an hour before you want to cook. Soak the lotus leaves in hot water for 1 hour, then pat them dry. Cover the rice with water and leave it to soak for 1 hour, then drain.

Soften the dried mushrooms by soaking them in hot water for 20–30 minutes. Squeeze out any excess water, remove the stems and chop the mushrooms finely.

Line a bamboo steamer with baking parchment or a cabbage leaf and add the drained rice. Half fill a wok or large saucepan with water – the steamer needs to sit above the water without touching. Place the steamer over the water and bring the water to the boil, then cover the rice and steam for about 20 minutes. Remove the rice, cover and keep warm while you prepare the rest of the ingredients.

Cut the chicken into small cubes about the size of a postage stamp and place them in a bowl. Cut the pork into pieces about the same size and add them to the same bowl. Then add the salt, a tablespoon of the rice wine and a teaspoon of the cornflour and leave the chicken and the pork to marinate for 20 minutes.

Put the remaining rice wine in a small bowl with the soy sauces. In a separate bowl, dissolve the remaining cornflour in a tablespoon of water, then whisk this into the wine and soy mix to make the sauce.

Place a wok on the heat and add the 2 tablespoons of vegetable oil. When the oil is hot, add the garlic and stir-fry until you can smell its aroma (about 30 seconds). Add the chicken cubes and pork and stir-fry until they turn white and are 80 per cent cooked through.

Add the sausages and the mushrooms and stir-fry for a minute. Give the sauce another quick stir, then add it to the middle of the pan, stirring quickly to thicken. Season with pepper to taste and cook for 1–2 more minutes to mix everything together and finish the cooking of the meat. Remove the pan from the heat, stir in the sesame oil and leave to cool.

Serves 8

4 lotus leaves, cut in half
200g glutinous rice
4 Chinese dried black mushrooms
cabbage leaves, for lining steamer (optional)
200g skinless chicken thighs,
100g pork loin, chopped into small pieces
¼ tsp salt
2 tbsp Shaoxing rice wine (or you can use dry sherry)
2 ½ tsp cornflour
1 tbsp light soy sauce
1 tsp dark soy sauce
2 tbsp vegetable oil, for stir-frying, or as needed
1 garlic clove, chopped
2 Chinese sausages (lap cheong), finely chopped
¼ tsp sesame oil
freshly ground black or white pepper

Divide both the rice and the filling into 8 equal portions. Lay a lotus leaf in front of you on your work surface. Place some of a portion of rice mixture on the centre of a lotus leaf and add a portion of filling on top, shaping the rice with your hands so that it forms a ring around the filling. Add the rest of that portion of rice to cover the filling.

Form a square parcel with the lotus leaf and tie it up with cooking twine. Repeat with the remaining lotus leaves and filling until you have 8 neat parcels and put them on a heatproof plate.

Place the plate of filled lotus leaves in a bamboo steamer over boiling water and steam for 15 minutes, or until they are heated through, then serve. (See the photo on the next page.)

SWEET AND SOUR FISH

A fab change from fish and chips – this is one of the nicest sweet and sour sauces we've made and the batter is beautifully crisp too. If you want something slightly fancier, you could blend the sauce and serve it with large fillets of battered fish instead of bite-sized pieces.

Place a wok or a large saucepan over a medium to high heat and add 2 tablespoons of groundnut oil. Once the oil is hot, add the chopped red onions, garlic and red pepper, then stir-fry for a couple of minutes or until the vegetables are just beginning to soften. Add the pineapple and the sugar and continue to stir-fry for 1 minute, by which time the sugar should have started to caramelise.

Turn up the heat and pour in the vinegar. Let it bubble up and then stir to help it mix with the melted sugar. Tip in the chopped tomatoes, soy sauce and fish sauce, then stir-fry for a further minute. Turn off the heat once the tomatoes have started to break down a little.

Tip the cornflour and the self-raising flour into a bowl. Pour in the lager, whisking constantly until you have a smooth batter. Season generously with salt and pepper.

Pour groundnut oil into a large deep-sided saucepan to a depth of about 10cm and heat to 180°C. Do not allow the oil to overheat and never leave hot oil unattended. It's best to fry your fish in batches so you don't overcrowd the pan. Drop the first batch of fish into the batter, then remove with tongs and carefully drop the pieces into the hot oil. Fry the fish for about 5 minutes, until the batter is crisp and has turned a very light shade of brown. Remove the fish from the oil with a slotted spoon and leave to drain on kitchen paper in a warm place, such as an oven on its lowest setting, while you fry the rest.

When you have fried all the fish, reheat the sauce and pour it on to a plate. Arrange your battered fish on top and finish with a flourish of red chilli. Serve up your deliciously different sweet and sour fish immediately, with some rice on the side.

Serves 4–6

groundnut oil, for frying
2 small red onions, roughly chopped
3 garlic cloves, finely chopped
1 red pepper, deseeded and chopped into 2cm chunks
¼ pineapple, peeled and cut into 2cm chunks
70g sugar
50ml red wine vinegar (cider or white wine vinegar are also fine)
2 tomatoes, roughly chopped
1 tbsp soy sauce
1 tsp fish sauce
100g cornflour
100g self-raising flour, plus a little extra for dusting
225ml light lager
750g skinless, thick white fish, such as sea bass or haddock, cut into 3cm chunks
1 red chilli, deseeded and finely sliced, for serving
flaked sea salt
freshly ground black pepper

TYPHOON MUSSELS

On a hot Sunday in Hong Kong we went out dragon boat racing. Afterwards, we went out with the victorious team and feasted on a fantastic seafood dish cooked on a sampan in the typhoon shelter in Hong Kong harbour. They used local crab, which was great, but we've come up with our own version of the recipe using mussels. Cheap and tasty – a real winner.

Scrub the mussels well and remove their beards. Chuck away any damaged mussels or those that don't close when you tap them on the work surface. Put the cleaned mussels in a colander and set aside.

Heat the olive oil in a large pan with a tight-fitting lid. Add the onion and cook slowly over a medium heat for 6–7 minutes or until soft and golden. Stir occasionally.

Add the ginger, garlic, and chilli and cook for a further minute until soft, then add the tomatoes and black beans and stir well. Tip the mussels into the pan and add the rice wine and soy sauce. Stir, then put the lid on and give the pan a good shake. Shake every minute or so until all the mussels have opened – this will probably take about 8 minutes.

Just before serving, gently fold in the spring onions, then divide the mussels between 2 large bowls and garnish with chopped coriander. Serve with some rice or crusty bread to mop up the juices.

Serves 2

1kg mussels
2 tbsp olive oil
1 onion, finely sliced
30g fresh root ginger, finely sliced
2 garlic cloves, finely sliced
1 large red chilli, deseeded and
    thinly sliced
2 tomatoes, skinned, deseeded
    and roughly chopped
2 tbsp fermented black beans,
    rinsed
75ml Shaoxing rice wine
1 tbsp soy sauce
2 spring onions, finely sliced
    at an angle
a small bunch of coriander,
    roughly chopped

WONTON NOODLE SOUP

Fragrant and nourishing, this is a feast of a soup – comfort food Hong Kong style. The wonton wrappers and noodles are crucial to the authentic flavour of this soup and this is our take on a real classic. Feel free to slurp when enjoying this soup. It would be rude not to!

Put the prawns on your chopping board and chop them finely until they are pretty much minced. Transfer them to a bowl and add the minced pork, chives, ginger, garlic, half of the sliced spring onions, half the sesame oil and half the soy sauce. Add plenty of white pepper, then mix well, until all the ingredients are well incorporated.

Place a wonton wrapper in front of you and put a large heaped teaspoon of the prawn and pork mixture into the middle of the wrapper. Wet your finger with a little water and run it around the edge of the wrapper, then gather up the sides of the wrapper around the filling and push together to seal. Lightly pinch the wrapper around the filling so that you are left with a tight ball topped with some excess wonton wrapper. Repeat the process with the remaining filling and wrappers.

Put a large saucepan of water on to boil. When the water is boiling, carefully drop in your wonton noodles and simmer for 3–4 minutes until they are just cooked. Drain the noodles and divide them between 2 bowls. Pour over the remaining sesame oil and soy sauce, then add the remaining sliced spring onions.

Bring a fresh saucepan of water to the boil, and at the same time begin heating your chicken stock in a separate pan. Once the water has boiled, add the filled wontons and cook for 3–4 minutes. Keep an eye on your stock and when it is close to boiling, add the oyster sauce and stir to dissolve. Don't let the stock boil.

When the wontons are cooked, remove them with a slotted spoon and divide them between the 2 bowls of noodles. Immediately pour over the hot stock, garnish with chopped chives if you like and serve at once.

Serves 2

8 raw king prawns, peeled and
    deveined (about 100g after
    peeling)
50g minced pork
2 tbsp chives, finely sliced
1cm piece of fresh root ginger,
    peeled and very finely chopped
1 garlic clove, very finely chopped
4 spring onions, finely sliced
4 tsp sesame oil
2 tbsp light soy sauce
12 wonton wrappers
    (round or square)
150g thin wonton noodles
600ml light chicken stock
1 tbsp oyster sauce
chopped chives, to garnish
    (optional)
freshly ground white pepper

CLAY POT DUCK WITH GINGER

We learned how to cook this at a street food stall in Hong Kong, using the traditional clay pot. It's fine to use an ordinary casserole dish or a sauté pan with a lid – the food will still taste great. You can get the clay pots here but you have to handle them carefully on the heat so they don't crack.

Put the mushrooms in a bowl of hot water to soak for 30 minutes. If using fresh shiitake mushrooms do not soak them.

Remove the skin from the duck breasts and cut them into bite-sized pieces. Mix together the soy sauce, sesame oil, rice wine, oyster sauce and cornflour to make a marinade. Stir everything well, then add the pieces of duck breast and stir until they are all well coated. Cover the bowl with cling film and leave the duck in the fridge to marinate for at least 30 minutes.

Once the mushrooms have finished soaking, drain and squeeze out the excess liquid. Using a sharp knife, thinly shred the wood ear mushrooms. Remove the stalks from the shiitake mushrooms and discard them, then cut the caps in half.

If you don't have a clay pot, use a casserole dish or sauté pan with a lid and place it on the hob. Heat 2 tablespoons of oil, add the ginger and cook until it has softened slightly. Push it to one side of the pot.

Remove the pieces of duck from the marinade and pat them dry with kitchen paper. Reserve the marinade liquid. Add the duck to the hot pot and fry to seal on all sides, then add the Sichuan pepper. Now add all the mushrooms, the garlic and chilli, then pour in the reserved marinade. Turn down the heat and cook for 10–12 minutes, depending on the size of the duck pieces and how well you like your duck cooked. Be careful not to cook the duck for too long, though, or it will be tough.

A couple of minutes before the end of the cooking time add the spring onions, choi sum, (or pak choi) and stir. Pop the lid on and cook until the greens are slightly wilted. Taste and adjust the seasoning if necessary – but remember that the soy sauce is salty so go easy. Garnish with the reserved slices of chilli before serving.

Serves 2

6 dried shiitake mushrooms (you can also use fresh)
2 large duck breasts
1 1/2 tbsp soy sauce
1/2 tsp sesame oil
1 tbsp Shaoxing rice wine
1 tbsp oyster sauce
1/2 tbsp cornflour
7g dried wood ear mushrooms
groundnut oil, for frying
25g fresh root ginger, cut into fine matchsticks
1/2 tsp ground Sichuan peppercorns
1 garlic clove, cut into slivers
1 red chilli, finely sliced (reserve 6–8 slices for the garnish)
2 spring onions, each cut into 3 at an angle
6 stems of fresh choi sum or some pak choi
flaked sea salt
freshly ground black pepper

STIR-FRIED TOMATOES AND EGGS
GRANDMA LULU STYLE

We were so happy to be invited to eat with Grandma Lulu and her family in their apartment in Hong Kong. This was real home cooking, food made with love and eaten with affection. Serve this dish on its own or with the five-spice belly pork on page 22 or even add a couple of bacon rashers for a bit of Lulu/Biker fusion.

Heat a wok on the hob and add a tablespoon of oil. When the oil is hot, add the eggs and scramble them quickly. Do not overcook. Remove the eggs from the wok and set aside.

Add the remaining tablespoon of oil to the wok, which should still be very hot, then fry the spring onions quickly. Add the chopped tomatoes and sugar and season with salt and pepper to taste.

When the tomatoes are cooked and their juices have made a sweet sauce, tip the eggs back into the pan. If the tomatoes seem a little dry, add a bit of water to loosen them. Let everything bubble for a minute then plate up!

Serves 2

2 tbsp groundnut or vegetable oil
1–2 eggs, beaten
2 spring onions, finely chopped
4 plum tomatoes, each chopped
   into 8 pieces
2 tsp grated palm sugar
1 tsp flaked sea salt
½ tsp freshly ground white pepper

SWEET AND SOUR PORK
GRANDMA LULU STYLE

Grandma Lulu could cook up a storm with a wok and a chopper. This is not sophisticated food but it's the way they cook sweet and sour at home in Hong Kong and it's dead tasty. One thing to mention – they butcher meat differently in Hong Kong and the ribs aren't as meaty. We hesitate to interfere with a great recipe but you might like to try this with pork shoulder, diced into 1cm cubes, for a meatier dish. Fresh pineapple works best but you can use canned if you like. Cut down the sugar though, if adding canned pineapple, as it's sweeter.

Wash the spare ribs and pat them dry with kitchen paper. Put them in a bowl with a sprinkling of salt, mix well and set aside for 15 minutes.

Meanwhile, beat the eggs in a bowl with the cornflour, then add enough water to make a smooth paste with the consistency of double cream.

Heat some groundnut oil to 180°C in a wok or use a deep-fat fryer. Don't let the oil overheat and never leave hot oil unattended. Dry the spare ribs with kitchen paper, dip them into the egg batter, then deep-fry in the hot oil until golden in colour and cooked through. Carefully remove the ribs from the pan and drain them on kitchen paper. Reserve the oil. All this can be done ahead of time if you like.

Place a wok on the hob and add a tablespoon of oil. Put the ribs in the pan, then add the ketchup, sugar and pineapple chunks and mix well. This is quite a dry dish so if you want more sauce, add a spoonful of pineapple juice if you have any, or use orange juice or water. Stir-fry until everything is heated through and serve piping hot.

Serves 2–4

1kg spare ribs, chopped
    into smaller pieces
2 eggs
2 tbsp cornflour
groundnut oil, for frying
3 tbsp tomato ketchup
4–6 tbsp sugar
4 fresh pineapple rings,
    chopped into chunks
flaked sea salt

BANGKOK AND CENTRAL THAILAND

If good food makes happy people, then Thailand is working. We've never been anywhere where people are as obsessed with food as they are in Thailand – it's a whole nation of people like us! They are always thinking and talking about food, planning the next meal while grazing on delicious little snacks.

For us, the highlight was the street food. Bangkok must be the street food capital of the world, with a bewildering array of incredible dishes available at every turn. Who needs to cook when you've got all that on your doorstep? And even the school dinners were great. We visited a school and discovered that everything was made from scratch every day, using the freshest ingredients. At 4.30 in the morning the head cook was in the market buying food for the day, and the kids ate like kings.

There are four basic flavours in Thai cooking – hot, salty, sweet and sour – and the balance of these in a dish is all-important. Seasonings are available on the table and we noticed even the schoolchildren helping themselves from pots of chillies, salt, sugar and lime to season their food. They knew just what to do and how their meal should taste.

Thai is probably our favourite food of all and we really wanted to get to the heart of Thai cooking. Characteristic ingredients are fragrant lemon grass and lime leaves, hot spicy chillies and aromatic herbs and it's all perfectly possible to cook at home. Stock up on some Thai flavours and share our passion for Thai food, with dishes such as pad Thai, green papaya salad and tom yum soup. You'll love them, we promise you.

CRISPY NOODLES WITH PRAWN AND CRAB

MEE KROB

We made this epic dish alongside the ruins of Ayutthaya, which was once the capital of old Siam as Thailand used to be called. The place was hot and exotic, just like this fine luxury salad. You can prepare everything in advance but keep the noodles, herbs, prawn and crab mix separate and put them all together at the last minute. The noodles are just dropped straight into the hot oil – no blanching needed. Bear in mind, though, that they do expand, so it's important to cook them in batches as we suggest.

First make the dressing. Mix the palm sugar and fish sauce until the sugar dissolves. Stir in the lime juice, then set aside.

Pour enough oil for deep-frying into a wok or a large deep saucepan and heat to 180–190°C. Don't allow the oil to overheat and never leave hot oil unattended. To test the temperature, add a small cube of bread. If the oil is hot enough, the bread will turn crisp and golden and float to the top in a few seconds. Fry the noodles in batches – each batch will cook in seconds. Add a batch to the pan and cook until the noodles are puffed up and turning a pale golden colour. Carefully remove the noodles with a slotted spoon and drain on kitchen paper. They'll look a bit like a giant haystack!

Wipe the wok and add 3 tablespoons of fresh oil, then fry the shallots until crispy. Remove them from the wok, drain on kitchen paper and set aside.

Put the wok back on the heat and add another tablespoon of vegetable oil. When the oil is hot, add the prawns and stir or toss them until they are slightly opaque. Add the ginger, garlic and galangal and sauté for a couple of minutes. Continue to cook and stir until the prawns are cooked. Tip the contents of the wok into a large bowl and add the crispy shallots.

Now add the spring onions, bean sprouts, lime leaves and crabmeat, then the dressing and the herbs. Mix everything together, but be gentle so you don't crush the herbs. We find that using our hands is best for this.

To serve, take a large bowl and layer the salad, starting with a layer of crispy noodles, then alternating layers of prawn and crab mixture and noodles. Garnish with slices of chilli and lime wedges and serve straight away.

Serves 4

vegetable or groundnut oil
125g thin rice noodles
5 Thai shallots (or 1 banana shallot),
    thinly sliced
400g raw, peeled tiger prawns,
    deveined
20g fresh root ginger, finely grated
3 garlic cloves, grated or crushed
20g galangal, finely grated
3 spring onions, cut lengthways
    and thinly sliced
150g fresh bean sprouts
3 kaffir lime leaves, finely sliced and
    cut into matchstick strips
200g fresh picked white crabmeat
big handful of fresh coriander,
    roughly chopped
big handful of mint, leaves picked
    from the stems (do not chop or
    the leaves will go brown)
big handful of holy basil

Dressing

2 heaped tbsp grated palm sugar

5 tbsp Thai fish sauce

3 tbsp fresh lime juice

Garnish

1 large red chilli, sliced at an angle

2 limes, cut into wedges

GREEN PAPAYA SALAD
SOM TUM

A Thai classic, this is a substantial salad that's tasty, sharp and spicy. It's great on its own or as a side dish with curry. Lime juice is an important ingredient so here's a top tip: roll the lime firmly with the palm of your hand over a work surface a few times before squeezing it and you'll get more juice. Simple, but it works. And always cut the lime through the middle, not end to end.

Put the garlic, ginger, lime juice, bird's-eye chilli, palm sugar, soy sauce, fish sauce and tamarind water in a pestle and mortar. Pound well to dissolve the sugar and mix all those lovely flavours, then tip everything into a large bowl.

Trim the beans and cut them into 5cm lengths. Bruise them slightly in the pestle and mortar, then add them to the bowl with the garlic, ginger and chilli dressing.

Cut the tomatoes in half and slightly bruise them in the pestle and mortar, then add them to the bowl with the beans.

Cut the papaya in half lengthways and remove the seeds. Using a mandolin or a sharp knife, cut the papaya flesh into fine matchstick strips and add them to the bowl. Drain the dried shrimps and add them to the salad, then mix well.

Pick the leaves from the mint and basil and toss them through the salad. Add the toasted peanuts and half the sliced red chilli and tip the salad into a large serving dish. Add the rest of the sliced chilli and serve. (See the photo on the next page.)

Serves 4

2 large garlic cloves, finely grated
20g fresh root ginger, finely grated
juice of 2 limes
1 red bird's-eye chilli, deseeded
    and finely chopped
3 tbsp grated palm sugar
2 tbsp soy sauce
4 tbsp Thai fish sauce
2 tbsp tamarind water
5 snake beans (or French beans)
10 cherry tomatoes
1 green papaya (about 700g)
1 large tbsp dried baby shrimps,
    soaked in boiling water for
    10 minutes
large bunch of fresh mint
    (about 30g)
large bunch of Thai basil
    (about 30g)
50g peanuts, toasted in a dry
    frying pan and roughly chopped
1 large red chilli, deseeded and
    finely sliced

SPICED CHICKEN AND PANDAN LEAVES
GAI HOR BAI TOEY

We cooked these in the street in Bangkok for a group of tuk-tuk drivers who fell on them as eagerly as they do on passengers. These tasty parcels are great served alongside the fishcakes and make a fantastic beer snack or starter. Pandan leaves are available from Asian supermarkets and online. They keep the chicken lovely and juicy and add a subtle nutty flavour. You'll need some cocktail sticks too for holding the little treasures together.

First make the sauce. Peel the root ginger and grate it finely into a bowl lined with muslin. Gather up the muslin and squeeze the juice from the ginger into the bowl, then discard the pulp. Add the remaining ingredients and mix well, then pour the sauce into a serving bowl, cover with cling film and set aside.

Cut the chicken breasts in half lengthways, then into bite-sized pieces.

Put the garlic cloves, coriander root and galangal in a small blender or food processor or a pestle and mortar. Add the palm sugar and blitz or pound to make a smooth paste. Tip the paste into a large mixing bowl and add the lime juice, sesame oil, Thai fish sauce, soy sauce and a good grinding of white pepper. Add the chicken pieces to the bowl and mix thoroughly so they're all covered with the marinade. Cover the bowl with cling film and leave to marinate in the fridge for half an hour.

While the chicken is marinating, bring a large pan of water to the boil. Gently ease in the pandan leaves, and blanch them for 30–40 seconds. Remove and pat them dry with some kitchen paper.

Remove the chicken from the fridge. Lay a blanched pandan leaf on the work surface and place a piece of chicken on the leaf, about 3cm from the end. Fold the pandan leaf over the chicken, then fold again in the same way. The next fold needs a little twist so that you cover the ends of the chicken that are sticking out and not already enclosed by the pandan leaf. Repeat these folds and rolls until the chicken is tucked up snugly in its pandan blanket and secure the ends with a cocktail stick. You should end up with a little bite-sized parcel of chicken entirely covered in pandan leaf. Repeat until you've used all the chicken.

Heat enough oil in a wok to deep fry or use a deep-fat fryer. Heat the oil to 180°C. Don't allow the oil to overheat and never leave hot oil unattended. Fry the chicken parcels in batches for 8 minutes or until the leaf takes on a golden hue. Remove with a slotted spoon and drain on kitchen paper. Serve with the sauce and wedges of lime. (See the photo on the next page.)

Makes about 20

500g skinless chicken breasts
4 garlic cloves, chopped
10g coriander root, washed and
    finely chopped
15g galangal, coarsely grated
1 tbsp crushed palm sugar
juice of 1 lime
1 tbsp sesame oil
1 tbsp Thai fish sauce
1 tbsp dark soy sauce
20 pandan leaves
vegetable oil, for frying
2 limes, cut into wedges, for serving
freshly ground white pepper

Sauce
40g fresh root ginger
pinch of sugar
1 tbsp sesame oil
½ tbsp Thai fish sauce
½ tbsp soy sauce
½ tbsp rice vinegar

THAI SEA BASS FISHCAKES WITH HONEY AND CUCUMBER DIP

Yes, these are from our book on curries but the Thai tuk-tuk drivers loved them so much we thought they deserved another outing. Great with sea bass as here, but they're fine made with cheaper white fish too. You can make your own red curry paste if you like, but you can get away with a good-quality bought one for this recipe. The secret to forming the quite sloppy mixture into cakes is to have wet hands – believe us, it works.

Trim the lemon grass, remove the outer leaves, then slice the tender inner part. Place the sea bass, fish sauce, red curry paste, lime leaf, galangal, lemon grass, chopped coriander, egg, palm sugar, beans and lime juice in a food processor and blitz to a paste. You'll need to remove the lid of the processor and push the mixture down with a spatula a few times. Carefully remove the blade of the processor and tip the mixture into a bowl.

Sprinkle a little flour on to a plate. Wet your hands, then take a walnut-sized piece of the mixture and roll it into a ball and flatten it into a thin disc. Lay the fishcake on a floured plate and make the rest in the same way until you've used all the mixture. Cover the fishcakes and chill them in the fridge until you're ready to cook.

Meanwhile, make the dip. Put the vinegar, honey, lime juice and fish sauce in a bowl, add 2 tablespoons of water and beat with a hand whisk. Taste and adjust the amount of honey and lime juice, depending on how sweet or sour you want the dip to be. Add the diced cucumber, carrot, shallot and sliced chillies – this dip is really more like a salsa.

Heat the oil in a large non-stick frying pan. Cook the fishcakes, a few at a time, for a couple of minutes, then turn and cook for another 2 minutes. They should be golden on both sides and cooked through.

For an extra flourish, serve the fishcakes on a banana leaf, with the dip in a little dish. Garnish the fishcakes with lamb's lettuce if you like. We like to drizzle the fishcakes with a little of the dip and pile some of the chunky bits on top. Yum, yum. (See the photo on the next page.)

Makes 18–20

1 lemon grass stalk
500g sea bass fillet, skinned and pin-boned
1 tbsp Thai fish sauce
2 tsp red curry paste
1 kaffir lime leaf, shredded
30g galangal, peeled and finely chopped
1 tbsp finely chopped fresh coriander
1 egg
1 tsp grated palm sugar
50g snake beans, trimmed and thinly sliced (or use fine green beans)
juice of ½ lime
plain flour, for dusting
3 tbsp vegetable oil, for shallow frying
banana leaf and lamb's lettuce, for serving (optional)

Dip
2 tbsp rice vinegar
2 tbsp runny honey
juice of ½ lime
1 tbsp Thai fish sauce
100g cucumber, peeled, deseeded and diced
1 small carrot, finely diced
1 shallot, finely diced
2 bird's-eye chillies, deseeded and finely sliced

SATAY KEBABS

Satay are a street food staple in Thailand, but they've become popular buffet fare in Britain and are not always as good as they should be. Prepared properly, satay are a thing of joy – juicy, spicy and tasty –and you can leave out the bird's-eye chilli if you don't like too much heat. You'll need a dozen 20cm wooden skewers.

First make the marinade. Put the garlic, shallots, lemon grass, chillies, galangal, palm sugar and turmeric in a mini blender or pestle and mortar. Blend or grind to a rough paste. Add the cumin, coriander, groundnut oil, dark soy sauce, fish sauce and a good grinding of black pepper, and blend or grind again to make a smooth paste. If using a food processor, you may need to push the paste down a couple of times with a rubber spatula. Tip into a large, non-metallic bowl.

Cut the beef or chicken into long, thin strips. If using pork fillet, cut it in half lengthways and then into long strips. Add your chosen meat (or prawns) to the marinade and mix well, then cover with cling film and leave to marinate in the fridge for at least 4–6 hours or preferably overnight.

Soak the wooden kebab sticks in water for at least half an hour so they don't burn when you cook the satay. When you're ready to cook, thread the pieces of meat or the prawns on to the skewers.

Heat a griddle pan on a medium to high heat and cook the satay in batches. There will be a bit of smoke from your griddle but don't worry – it's just getting up to temperature. Beef satay will take 1–2 minutes on each side. Chicken, pork and prawns will both need 3–4 minutes on each side – check that the meat is cooked through, with no pinkness remaining. Serve with satay sauce and lime wedges. The pickled cucumber salad goes well too. (See the photo on the previous page.)

Satay sauce
Put the peanut butter, coconut cream, garlic, tamarind paste, chilli and soy sauce in a small pan. Place over a medium heat and stir slowly and continuously as it heats, then simmer for 30 seconds. Remove from the heat, add the lime juice and taste for seasoning. Pour into a heatproof serving bowl and set aside until ready to serve.

Pickled cucumber salad
Dissolve the sugar in the vinegar, then add the cucumber, shallots and chilli and mix well. Set aside for about 30 minutes before serving to allow the flavours to infuse.

Makes 12

2 x 225g beef sirloin steak, about
    2cm thick
or 2 x 225g boneless, skinless
    chicken breasts
or 1 pork fillet (tenderloin)
or 400g large raw peeled prawns,
    deveined
2 limes, cut into wedges, for serving

Marinade
3 garlic cloves, roughly chopped
6 Thai shallots (or 2 banana
    shallots), roughly chopped
2 lemon grass stalks, trimmed and
    white part finely sliced
1 large red chilli, deseeded and
    roughly chopped
1 red bird's-eye chilli, deseeded
    and roughly chopped (optional)
20g galangal (or fresh root ginger),
    grated
1 1/2 tsp crushed palm sugar
2.5cm piece of fresh turmeric
    root, finely grated or 1 1/2 tsp
    powdered turmeric
1 1/2 tsp ground cumin
2 tsp ground coriander
2 tbsp groundnut oil
2 tbsp dark soy sauce
1 tbsp Thai fish sauce
freshly ground black pepper

Satay sauce

125g crunchy peanut butter
1 x 165ml can of coconut cream
1 garlic clove, finely grated
    or crushed
½ tsp tamarind paste
1 large dried red chilli, soaked in
    warm water for 10 minutes
    then finely shredded
2 tbsp soy sauce
juice of ½ lime
flaked sea salt
freshly ground black pepper

Pickled cucumber salad (optional)

1 tsp crushed palm sugar
50ml rice vinegar
½ cucumber, cut into small dice
4 Thai shallots (or 1 banana shallot),
    sliced
1 red bird's-eye chilli, deseeded
    and chopped (optional)

THAI BEEF STIR-FRY

We thought stir-fries would be everywhere in Bangkok, but they were not as common as we thought. The ones we did eat were wonderfully fragrant though, such as this feast of spicy beef, which is served with a crispy fried egg for a mega-satisfying meal.

First make the sauce. Put the coriander roots, garlic and chillies in a pestle and mortar and crush them lightly. Add the remaining sauce ingredients and give them all a good pound to infuse the flavours, then tip the sauce into a small serving bowl. Don't wash the pestle and mortar – you want the residue of lovely flavours for the next stage.

Add the bird's-eye chillies, garlic and sea salt to the pestle and mortar and pound to form a paste.

Place a wok on a medium heat and when it's hot, add 3 tablespoons of vegetable oil. Stir-fry the sliced shallots for 3–4 minutes until golden. Turn down the heat, add the chilli and garlic paste and cook for about a minute or until lightly brown. Keep stirring so the garlic doesn't burn.

Whack up the heat, add the beef and the finely diced red pepper and cook for 4–5 minutes or until the beef is nearly done.

Meanwhile, heat a large frying pan with 2 tablespoons of vegetable oil. Fry the eggs until the edges of the whites are crispy but the yolks are still runny.

To the wok, add the fish sauce, oyster sauce, soy sauce and palm sugar and mix thoroughly. Lastly, add the basil leaves and fold them through the cooked beef. Spoon the beef into bowls and top with a fried egg, then serve at once with some rice and sauce on the side.

Serves 3–4

4 bird's-eye chillies, deseeded
    and roughly chopped
4 garlic cloves, roughly chopped
½ tsp flaked sea salt
vegetable oil
10 Thai shallots (or 3 banana
    shallots), finely sliced
700g sirloin or rib of beef,
    coarsely chopped
1 small red pepper, deseeded
    and finely diced
4 eggs
2 tbsp Thai fish sauce
1 tbsp oyster sauce
2 tbsp soy sauce
1 ½ tbsp palm sugar
a good handful of Thai basil and a
    smaller handful of holy basil
freshly cooked rice, for serving

Sauce
4 coriander roots, finely chopped
2 garlic cloves, finely chopped
5 chillies, deseeded and finely
    chopped
1 tbsp oyster sauce
1 tbsp rice vinegar
2 tbsp soy sauce
2 tbsp Thai fish sauce
juice of ½ lime

THAI FISH BALL NOODLE SOUP

The Cantonese have their wonton noodle soup but here is a Thai version, made with awesome little fish balls instead of dumplings and a fabulously fragrant broth. This makes a complete meal in a bowl that's tasty, light and very satisfying. Try it and you'll see what we mean. By the way, piercing the chillies releases most of the heat – but not the seeds – and all of the flavour.

First make the soup. Place all the ingredients for the soup in a large saucepan. Bring it to the boil, then reduce the heat to a simmer and cook gently for 15 minutes. Strain the stock through a sieve into a bowl, discard the debris and tip the liquid into a clean pan. Set aside until ready to use.

Put all the ingredients for the fish balls in a food processor. Pulse gently until the mixture forms a firm paste but still retains a little texture.

Put a bowl of cold water on your work surface, wet your hands and shape a tablespoon of the mixture into a ball a little smaller than a golf ball. Place it on a plate, wet your hands again and continue until you've made 16 fish balls and used all the mixture. Put the fish balls in the fridge until you are ready to use them.

Put the rice noodles in a bowl of just-boiled water and leave them to soak for about 10 minutes.

Place the pan of soup back on the heat and bring it to the boil, then reduce the heat to a gentle simmer. Gently place the fish balls into the simmering stock and cook them for 8 minutes.

While the fish balls are cooking, take 4 large serving bowls and place a quarter of the bean sprouts, a quarter of the pak choi, a quarter of the chives and a quarter of the hot noodles in each bowl. Place 4 fish balls on each serving and ladle over the hot stock. Add a lime wedge and some basil and serve at once.

Serves 4

Soup

2 litres good chicken stock (shop-bought or home-made)
30g fresh root ginger, peeled and cut into slivers
2 lemon grass stalks, bashed and bruised
2 bird's-eye chillies, pierced with the tip of a sharp knife
2 whole star anise
4 kaffir lime leaves
2 tbsp roughly chopped palm sugar
3 tbsp Thai fish sauce
1 tbsp soy sauce

Fish balls

500g firm white fish, such as cod, pollock, haddock, whiting or sea bass
1 tbsp Thai fish sauce
3 kaffir lime leaves, finely shredded
2 garlic cloves, finely grated or crushed
1 small handful of fresh coriander
1 tsp sesame oil
½ tsp freshly ground white pepper
1 egg white
2 tbsp rice flour

Garnish

200g thin rice noodles
200g bean sprouts
12 garlic chives (ordinary chives would do), trimmed and cut into 5cm pieces
20 baby pak choi or 4 smallish ones cut into quarters
1 lime, cut into quarters
small handful of Thai basil

TOM YUM SOUP

Traditionally, this is the nuclear reactor of the soup world. It's super-spicy and addictive but cut down on the chilli if you can't stand the heat. Once you get the taste for it – like we have – there's no going back. The chilli paste is really versatile and can be served with chicken, fish or grilled veg. The paste recipe makes more than you need for the soup but it keeps for a couple of weeks in the fridge.

Peel and devein the prawns, keeping the heads and shells. Put the heads and shells in a medium saucepan and add the chicken stock, 1 crushed lemon grass stalk and 3 of the lime leaves. Bring to the boil, then turn the heat down to a simmer and cook for a good 10 minutes. Strain the stock through a sieve into another medium pan and, using the back of a spoon, crush the shells and heads to extract as much flavour and liquid as possible.

Put the saucepan of stock back on the heat and slowly bring it to a simmer. Add the remaining stick of lemon grass, finely sliced, the rest of the lime leaves and the galangal, chillies, palm sugar, 2 tablespoons of chilli paste, the fish sauce, coconut cream or milk and soy sauce. Cook for a further 10 minutes to infuse all the flavours.

Add the peeled prawns and button mushrooms and cook for about 4 minutes, or until the prawns have turned pink and are cooked through. Add the sliced scallops, cherry tomatoes and lime juice – the heat of the stock will cook the scallops. Tip the soup into serving bowls and garnish with the basil or coriander.

Roasted chilli paste

Place a large non-stick frying pan or wok over a medium heat. Roast the chillies in a dry pan until they turn a medium dark brown – this should take about 5 minutes. Toss the chillies from time to time so they brown evenly. Tip the roasted chillies into a food processor or pestle and mortar and put the pan back on the heat.

Add 2 tablespoons of oil to the pan and gently fry the garlic cloves over a medium heat until they are golden brown and soft. Add the garlic to the chillies and put the pan back on the heat. Add another 2 tablespoons of oil to the pan and gently fry the sliced shallots until golden brown and soft, then add them to the chillies and garlic. It's important to fry these separately as the garlic takes longer to cook.

Add the remaining ingredients to the food processor or pestle and mortar and blend or pound them to a smooth paste. If using a food processor, you might need to remove the lid and push the mixture down a couple of times with a rubber spatula until the consistency is right.

Serves 4

1kg medium-large raw tiger prawns
1.5 litres chicken stock
2 lemon grass stalks
7 kaffir lime leaves
30g galangal, sliced into 4 pieces
3–4 bird's-eye chillies
3 tsp crushed palm sugar
2 large tbsp roasted chilli paste
(see recipe below)
2 tbsp Thai fish sauce
160ml coconut cream or thick
coconut milk
1 tbsp soy sauce
12 button mushrooms, halved
4 large scallops, each sliced in half
horizontally
12 cherry tomatoes, halved
juice of 2 limes
Thai basil or fresh coriander,
to garnish

Roasted chilli paste

40g dried red chillies
vegetable or groundnut oil,
for frying
20 large garlic cloves, roughly
chopped
16 Thai shallots (or 4 banana
shallots), sliced
2 large tbsp dried shrimps
6 tbsp grated palm sugar or
soft brown sugar
4 tbsp Thai fish sauce
juice of 2 limes

AUNTIE DAENG'S GREEN CURRY

Chef Chanchavee Skulkant, who everyone calls Auntie Daeng, is famous in Thailand for having cooked for the Thai royal family. Now she runs a little restaurant in Bangkok serving up the most amazing traditional food at very reasonable prices. This is her green curry recipe which is straightforward and so good. Apple aubergines are smaller than the ones we're used to and you can find them in Asian stores. You can also use pea aubergines which are smaller still. Make the curry paste before you tackle the recipe.

For the curry, place a wok on the heat and add a tablespoon of vegetable oil. Add 50g of the curry paste and stir-fry, then add 200ml of the coconut milk. Continue to stir-fry until the pan is almost dry, then add another 200ml of coconut milk. Repeat until all the milk has been used.

Add the meat or fish to the pan, stir, then add the coconut cream. Cover the pan until the mixture comes to the boil, then add the fish sauce, palm sugar, aubergines (or aubergine pieces), green chillies and lime leaves. Cook until the aubergines are soft and the meat or fish is cooked. Garnish with Thai basil and serve with rice.

Green curry paste
To make the paste, put the coriander and cumin seeds in a pestle and mortar with the peppercorns and crush them. Tip them out and add the green chillies and salt to the pestle and mortar and pound to make a paste.

Add the galangal, lemon grass, lime rind and coriander root and continue to pound. Mix in the crushed seeds, then the garlic, shallots and shrimp paste and pound everything to a paste. Those of us with less energy than Auntie Daeng could do this in a food processor.

Serves 4

vegetable oil
50g green curry paste (see below)
600ml coconut milk
400g chicken, pork, beef, fish
   or raw prawns
50g coconut cream, grated
3 tbsp Thai fish sauce
2 tbsp grated palm sugar
5 apple aubergines
2 long green Thai chillies,
   deseeded and chopped
6 kaffir lime leaves, cut into very
   thin strips
handful of Thai basil, torn
Thai rice, for serving

Green curry paste
1 tbsp coriander seeds
1 tsp cumin seeds
1 tsp dry white peppercorns
15 green chillies (add a small
   amount first and taste, as
   they vary in heat)
1 tsp salt
1 tsp finely chopped galangal
1 tbsp crushed lemon grass
½ tsp grated kaffir lime zest or
   ordinary lime zest
1 tsp grated coriander root
9 garlic cloves, crushed
3 Thai shallots (or 1 banana shallot),
   finely chopped
1 tsp shrimp paste

AUNTIE DAENG'S STIR-FRIED CRAB WITH YELLOW CHILLIES

Another cracking recipe from Auntie Daeng's restaurant in Bangkok. Again, this is simple and straightforward but really delicious. Go carefully with the chillies and taste before you add them all in case it gets too hot for you. And if you can't find yellow chillies, you can use mild red ones. Rice bran oil is available here and is good for stir-frying as it has a high smoking point and a mild flavour, but you can use groundnut oil instead.

Bring a saucepan of water to the boil. Add the beans, boil for one minute, then drain and refresh them in cold water.

Put the yellow chillies and garlic in a pestle and mortar and pound them to make a rough paste.

Place a wok over the heat and add the oil. Stir-fry the pounded garlic and chillies for a couple of minutes – you'll start to smell the garlicky aroma and the garlic will turn yellow.

Add the fish sauce, palm sugar and beans. Then add the crabmeat, turn down the heat and stir fry gently to heat through without breaking up the crab. Serve at once.

Serves 2–3

5 snake beans, cut into 1cm pieces
50g long yellow chillies
4 garlic cloves, peeled
1 tbsp rice bran oil
    (or groundnut oil)
2 tbsp Thai fish sauce
1 tsp grated palm sugar
200g crabmeat from a large
    cooked crab

PAD THAI

This is a classic Thai dish and it's one of the best. Yes, there are a lot of ingredients here but there's nothing difficult and as long as you get everything ready, cut and mixed before you start cooking it's a breeze. Once all that's done it's quick to cook and needs eating at once so have your family and friends lined up and ready to enjoy their feast. If you like, you could use chicken or queen scallops instead of crab.

Beat the eggs in a small bowl with the spring onions and a tablespoon of the fish sauce. Season with salt and pepper, then set aside.

Strain the tamarind through a small sieve into a separate bowl and discard any pulp. Add the palm sugar and the remaining fish sauce, then mix well to dissolve the sugar. Set aside.

Place a large wok on a medium to high heat and add 2 tablespoons of oil. Add the tofu cubes and fry until they're golden brown on all sides. Remove them gently with a slotted spoon and set aside on a plate lined with kitchen paper. Put the wok back on the heat and add another tablespoon of oil. Add the ginger, lemon grass, chillies, shallots and garlic and cook gently for a couple of minutes. Add the prawns and cook until they are just pink and nearly done, then add the tamarind mix.

Place a large frying pan over a medium heat with 2 tablespoons of vegetable oil. Pour in the eggs and swirl the pan so the eggs coat the bottom of the pan and cook until you have a super-thin omelette. You will only need to cook this on one side, as it's so thin, but make sure the base has a little colour. Turn the omelette out on to a plate, slice it into strips and set aside.

Drain the noodles and add them to the wok with the crab, bean sprouts, dried shrimps, chives, a small handful of Thai basil, coriander leaves and the reserved cooked tofu. Stir in the strips of omelette and quickly toss all the ingredients together to heat through.

Garnish with the chopped roasted peanuts, roasted chilli flakes, reserved chive flowers and some wedges of lime.

In Bangkok they sometimes serve this a different way, keeping the omelette whole and rolling the filling up in it to make a handy street food snack.

Serves 2–4

2 large eggs
3 spring onions, thinly sliced at
    an angle
3 tbsp Thai fish sauce
1 tsp tamarind paste, dissolved
    in 25ml boiling water
2 heaped tbsp grated palm sugar
vegetable or groundnut oil
125g firm tofu, cut into 12 cubes
30g fresh root ginger, peeled
    and finely grated
1 lemon grass stalk, white part
    finely sliced
2 red bird's-eye chillies, deseeded
    and finely chopped
4 Thai shallots (or 1 banana shallot),
    thinly sliced
2 large garlic cloves, finely chopped
    or grated
150g raw, peeled tiger prawns,
    deveined and roughly chopped

100g medium rice noodles, placed
   in a large bowl and covered with
   boiling water
100g fresh white crabmeat
75g bean sprouts
15g dried shrimps, chopped
10 Chinese chives, cut into 5cm
   lengths (keep the flowers to
   garnish the dish) or a small
   handful of chives
leaves from a small handful of
   Thai basil
fresh coriander leaves, chopped
flaked sea salt
freshly ground black pepper

Garnish
50g roasted peanuts, roughly
   chopped
1 tsp chilli flakes, roasted in a dry pan
chive flowers (see above)
1 lime, cut into wedges

THAI VEGETABLE CURRY

What makes this curry special is the home-made red curry paste. Once you get the ingredients together it's made in no time and it will turn your curry into a thing of beauty. While you're at it, you might as well make a big batch – this recipe will give you far more than you need for this curry. Spoon it into a sterilised jar, seal tightly and keep it in the fridge for up to one month. Alternatively, put the paste in ice cube trays and freeze for up to three months.

Heat a tablespoon of the vegetable oil in a large wok over a high heat. When the oil is smoking, add the leek, garlic and chilli and stir-fry for 3–5 minutes, or until softened but not browned. Add the 2 tablespoons of curry paste and fry for 2–3 minutes, stirring well.

Add the lime leaves, carrots and chopped tomatoes, then pour in the coconut milk and vegetable stock and stir well to combine. Bring the mixture to the boil, then reduce the heat until simmering and continue to simmer, uncovered, for about 10 minutes.

Add the cauliflower florets, butternut squash, beans and bamboo shoots and continue to simmer for 12–15 minutes, or until the butternut squash is tender and the sauce has thickened slightly and reduced.

When the vegetables in the curry are tender and the sauce has thickened, stir in the chopped coriander. To serve, spoon the rice into bowls, ladle over the vegetable curry and garnish with a few bean sprouts.

Thai red curry paste
For the Thai red curry paste, put all the ingredients in a food processor and blitz to a smooth paste. You'll need to remove the lid and push the mixture down a couple of times with a rubber spatula until you get the right consistency.

Thai sticky rice
Before starting to make the curry, soak the sticky rice in cold water for at least 20 minutes, or up to 3 hours.

Drain the soaked rice and rinse it thoroughly. Punch a few holes in a sheet of baking paper and use it to line a metal or bamboo steamer. Add the drained rice to the steamer, cover tightly and suspend the steamer over a pan of boiling water for 20 minutes. Don't let the bottom of the steamer touch the surface of the water.

Serves 4

2 tbsp vegetable oil
1 large leek, trimmed, thinly sliced
2 garlic cloves, crushed to a paste
1 large red chilli, deseeded and finely chopped
2 tbsp Thai red curry paste (see recipe)
4 kaffir lime leaves
2 carrots, peeled and roughly chopped
1 x 400g can of chopped tomatoes
400g coconut milk
250ml vegetable stock
1 small cauliflower, trimmed and cut into florets
½ small butternut squash, peeled, deseeded, flesh cut into 2.5cm pieces
175g snake or French beans, trimmed
1 x 225g can of bamboo shoots, drained
bunch of fresh coriander, chopped
handful of fresh bean sprouts, for serving

Thai red curry paste

4 small red onions, roughly chopped

16 garlic cloves, peeled

12 lemon grass stalks, outer leaves removed, white part roughly chopped

8 large red chillies, stems removed

8 tbsp chopped fresh coriander (roots and leaves)

8 tsp chilli powder

10cm piece of fresh galangal, peeled

4 tsp grated lime zest

4 kaffir lime leaves

4 tsp shrimp paste

12 tsp hot paprika

8 tsp ground turmeric

2 tsp cumin seeds

8 tbsp vegetable oil

Thai sticky rice

250g glutinous rice

THAI CURRY PUFFS

Diet food these are not, but man, they're good, with meltingly flaky pastry encasing a delectable filling. We've used chicken and sweet potato but you can vary this as you like. True, these do take a bit of work but you can make the filling in advance. We ate them at a market stall in Bangkok and couldn't wait to try our own version.

First make the filling. Place a wok or sauté pan on the heat and add the 2 tablespoons of oil. Add the diced chicken and onion and fry until the chicken has lost its rawness and the onion is translucent. Add the curry paste and curry powder and continue to cook for a couple of minutes.

Add the sweet potato cubes, then the condensed milk, sea salt and black pepper. Stir gently. Bring everything to the boil, then crumble in the stock cube, turn down the heat and simmer for 10-12 minutes until the sweet potato is soft and the sauce has begun to reduce. Mix the cornflour with 2 tablespoons of water in a small bowl, then add it to the pan. Cook for another minute or so until the cornflour has thickened the sauce. Once cooked, set aside to cool completely before you make the puffs.

Now make the water dough. In a jug, dissolve the sugar and salt in the lukewarm water and set aside. Put the flour into a food processor, whizz to aerate the flour then add the vegetable oil. Next add the sesame seeds, then slowly pour in the sugared water while the machine is running until the dough comes together. You may not need all the sugared water – the dough should be tacky but not wet. Form the dough into a ball with your hands and then wrap it in cling film and put it in the fridge to rest and chill for 30 minutes.

For the oil dough, put the flour and salt in a food processor, whizz to aerate, then break in the lard or suet. Blitz until it becomes a tacky dough. If it is still dry add a tablespoon of water to get the tackiness. It should not be wet. Form into a ball with your hands and wrap it in cling film and chill for 30 minutes.

Now make your puffs. Dust the surface with flour. Take the ball of water dough and roll it out into a rectangle (about 35 x 25cm). Shape the oil dough into a small rectangular block (about 12 x 8cm) and place this on top of the water dough. Fold over the edges, like you're wrapping a parcel, and then pinch the seams to seal. Turn the seam side downwards. Dust the surface again, and shape the dough into a rectangle until it is about 4mm thick (the thinner the better, as you get a better flaky pastry). Pinch out any air bubbles that may form. You should have a rectangle that measures about 45 x 35cm.

Makes up to 18 large or 30 small puffs

Filling
2 tbsp vegetable oil
500g boneless chicken thigh or breast, finely diced
1 medium onion, finely diced
2 tbsp massaman curry paste (shop-bought or see p. 105)
2 tbsp curry powder
1 medium sweet potato (about 400g), peeled and finely diced
1 x 397g can of condensed milk
2 tsp flaked sea salt
1 tsp cracked black pepper
1 chicken stock cube
1 tbsp cornflour

Water dough
1 tbsp sugar
½ tsp salt
125ml lukewarm water
300g plain flour, plus extra for dusting
4 tbsp vegetable oil
2 tbsp black sesame seeds (optional)

Oil dough
200g plain flour
½ tsp salt
125g lard or vegetable suet

Take the top edge of the dough and roll it up very tightly down towards you, like a Swiss roll. Wrap it in cling film and chill for 15 minutes.

Dust the surface well with flour again, put the dough horizontally in front of you and roll it back into a rectangle about the same size as before. Again, take the top end and roll it up very tightly into a Swiss roll. Wrap the dough in cling film and leave it to rest in the fridge for another 15 minutes.

Once the pastry has rested, take the roll and place it in front of you. Trim both ends (save them to test the heat of the oil), then cut the remaining roll into 18 equal slices. On a lightly floured surface gently roll each disc until it is 15cm in diameter. The pastry can be quite sticky so keep the surface and the rolling pin floured to avoid lifting the spiral out. You may also need to shape the dough while rolling to keep the shape.

Place a good tablespoon of the filling mixture in the centre of each round of pastry. Make sure you have enough space to be able to seal the pastry over the mixture and be able to form a half crescent with about 1.5cm of lip.

Pinch and twist the pastry, starting at one end and working over to the other to form a pleated or roped edge in the same way as you would with a Cornish pasty.

Half fill a large saucepan with oil or use a deep-fat fryer. Heat the oil to 180°C. Don't allow the oil to overheat and never leave hot oil unattended. You can use the pastry trimmings to check the heat of the oil – if the pieces go brown in 30 seconds the oil is hot enough.

Do not overcrowd the pan. Cook the puffs in batches, 2 or 3 at a time, for 8–10 minutes until golden all over and puffed up. Drain on kitchen paper and serve the puffs hot or warm.

Mini puffs make perfect snacks for parties. Make them in the same way but cut the roll of dough into about 30 equal discs and place a smaller amount of mixture in the centre of each round. You can make these in advance, up to the point of frying, and freeze them until the day you need them.

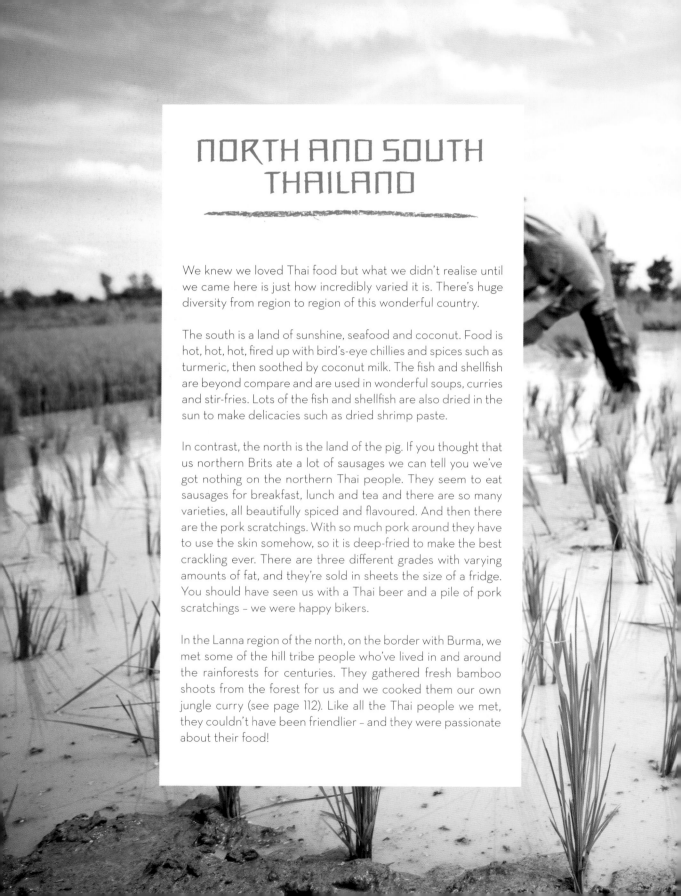

NORTH AND SOUTH THAILAND

We knew we loved Thai food but what we didn't realise until we came here is just how incredibly varied it is. There's huge diversity from region to region of this wonderful country.

The south is a land of sunshine, seafood and coconut. Food is hot, hot, hot, fired up with bird's-eye chillies and spices such as turmeric, then soothed by coconut milk. The fish and shellfish are beyond compare and are used in wonderful soups, curries and stir-fries. Lots of the fish and shellfish are also dried in the sun to make delicacies such as dried shrimp paste.

In contrast, the north is the land of the pig. If you thought that us northern Brits ate a lot of sausages we can tell you we've got nothing on the northern Thai people. They seem to eat sausages for breakfast, lunch and tea and there are so many varieties, all beautifully spiced and flavoured. And then there are the pork scratchings. With so much pork around they have to use the skin somehow, so it is deep-fried to make the best crackling ever. There are three different grades with varying amounts of fat, and they're sold in sheets the size of a fridge. You should have seen us with a Thai beer and a pile of pork scratchings – we were happy bikers.

In the Lanna region of the north, on the border with Burma, we met some of the hill tribe people who've lived in and around the rainforests for centuries. They gathered fresh bamboo shoots from the forest for us and we cooked them our own jungle curry (see page 112). Like all the Thai people we met, they couldn't have been friendlier – and they were passionate about their food!

CUCUMBER SALAD
YUM TANG GWA

A lovely fresh-tasting salad, this makes a great accompaniment to richer dishes, such as those with coconut milk. It looks as pretty as a picture too.

To make the dressing, mix all the ingredients together in a bowl. Stir well, making sure that the palm sugar has dissolved and the ingredients are thoroughly mixed. Set aside for the flavours to develop.

Using a potato peeler, peel the cucumber lengthways in long strips, leaving a little skin between each strip for a stripy effect. Cut the cucumber in half lengthways and remove the seeds. The easiest way to do this is to run a dessert spoon down the centre, scooping out the seeds. Cut each half into slices the thickness of a pound coin – they should look like little half-moons. Place the cucumber slices in a large mixing bowl.

Add the spring onions, chillies, shallots and peanuts, then the chopped herbs. Pour on the dressing, mix well and serve.

If you like, you can get all the ingredients for this salad ready in advance but it's best to add the herbs and dressing at the last minute.

Serves 4 as a side dish

1 large cucumber
4 spring onions, trimmed and
    sliced at an angle
2 red bird's-eye chillies, deseeded
    and thinly sliced
10 Thai shallots (or 2–3 banana
    shallots), thinly sliced
50g peanuts, toasted and roughly
    chopped
large handful of fresh coriander,
    roughly chopped
large handful of mint leaves,
    roughly chopped

Dressing
4 tbsp rice vinegar
5 tbsp Thai fish sauce
1 ½ tbsp grated palm sugar
juice of 1 lime

STIR-FRIED CHICKEN AND BASIL
GAI PAO GRAPOW

This is a quick version of a chicken and basil dish that was cooked for us by a home cook in Bangkok. It's a classic and very tasty so big thanks to Chow's family for the inspiration. The nam pla prik dressing is on every table in Thailand. It's quick as a flash to make but tastes the business.

To make the nam pla prik dressing, mix all the ingredients together in a small bowl, then set aside.

Place a wok on the heat and add the groundnut oil. When the oil is warm, add the shallots, chillies and garlic and cook over a medium heat until soft, taking care not to let anything burn. This will take 4–6 minutes.

Turn up the heat, add the chicken and cook until it is all lightly browned. Keep breaking the chicken up with the back of a wooden spoon and toss it from time to time so it all cooks evenly. Add the lime leaves, beans and fish sauce and cook for a further 3–4 minutes, until the beans are lightly cooked but still crunchy. Add the soy sauce and a handful of basil and mix thoroughly.

Serve immediately with the nam pla prik dressing on the side and heaps of steamed or boiled rice.

Serves 4

2 tbsp groundnut oil
8 Thai shallots, finely sliced
4 red bird's-eye chillies, deseeded and finely chopped (adjust quantity to taste as this is quite hot!)
6 garlic cloves, finely chopped
600g boneless, skinless, chicken thighs, finely chopped
4 kaffir lime leaves
12 snake beans or a handful of French beans, cut into 4cm lengths
6 tbsp Thai fish sauce
1 tbsp sweet soy sauce
large handful of Thai basil

Nam pla prik dressing
1 bird's-eye red chilli, deseeded and very finely sliced
1 bird's-eye green chilli, deseeded and very finely sliced
1 Thai shallot, very finely diced
75ml Thai fish sauce

HOT AND SPICY SQUID SALAD
YAM PRA MUEK

This is a quick spice hit that really captures the flavours of Thailand. Squid is readily available and goes brilliantly with chilli – it's a great marriage of texture and taste. You can ask your fishmonger to clean the squid for you but it's easy to do yourself so follow our guidelines below.

To make the dressing, put all the ingredients in a pestle and mortar and pound to incorporate all the flavours. Set aside until needed.

If you're cleaning the squid yourself, cut off the tentacles, then pull the innards out of the body. Make sure you remove the quill, which looks like a bit of plastic, then discard the innards and the quill. Pull the purplish membrane off the body and chuck it away. Rinse the tentacles and pull out the little hard beak from the centre, then cut the tentacles into halves or quarters.

Slit the body cones along one side and open them out. Rinse them well to remove any remaining innards. Score the inside in a criss-cross pattern with the tip of a knife, working diagonally across the flesh without cutting all the way through – always cut from the inside, as this will allow the squid to curl during cooking. Cut each cone in half and pat all the squid dry with kitchen paper.

Cut the cucumber in half lengthways. Using a spoon, scrap the seeds out of the centre and chuck them away, then cut the cucumber into 5mm slices. Put the slices in a large bowl with the garlic, chives, spring onions, shallots and tomatoes, then add the mint leaves and basil.

Place a wok or a large frying pan on the heat and add the vegetable and sesame oils. Once the oils are hot, add the ginger and fry until it is just turning golden brown. Add the squid and tentacles and cook for another 1½ minutes, until the squid has curled up and is just cooked. Add the dressing to the hot squid and toss well, then tip the contents of the wok into the bowl with the salad. Mix thoroughly and serve straight away with lime wedges.

Serves 4

400g small squid (including tentacles)
½ cucumber
1 large garlic clove, finely chopped
20 garlic chives with flowers or a bunch of chives, cut into 2.5cm lengths
5 spring onions, trimmed, cut in half and quartered lengthways
5 Thai shallots (or 1–2 banana shallots), finely sliced
20 cherry tomatoes, halved
20g fresh mint, leaves picked from the stems
handful of Thai basil
2 tbsp vegetable oil
1 tbsp sesame oil
30g fresh root ginger, peeled and cut into matchstick strips
lime wedges, for serving

Dressing

3 red bird's-eye chillies, deseeded and finely chopped
1 garlic clove, finely chopped
2 heaped tbsp grated palm sugar
2 tbsp Thai fish sauce
juice of ½ lime

SPICED MINCED CHICKEN
LAAB GAI

We ate particularly good versions of this dish in Chiang Mai, northern Thailand, and we've come up with this recipe. You can make it with minced pork if you like and vary the chillies in the dressing to make it as hot, or not, as you like. Some of the dishes we had practically made our eyes bleed. There are lots of other lovely subtle flavours as well so even if you do scale down the chillies, your laab gai will still be delicious.

To make the dressing, put all the ingredients in a pestle and mortar and give them a good pound to combine all the flavours. Set aside.

Put the chicken in a bowl with the lime juice and leave it to marinate for 5 minutes.

Place a wok on the heat, add the uncooked sticky rice and dry roast it until it's golden brown – we know this sounds a bit odd, but trust us. Tip the roasted rice into a pestle and mortar or a spice grinder and grind to make a coarse powder, then set aside. Now add the peanuts to the wok and toast them slowly until golden brown, then set aside. You'll be using the wok again so there's no need to wash it out at this stage.

Heat the vegetable oil in the wok over a medium heat and add the marinated chicken. Fry the chicken until it's cooked through and no pinkness remains, breaking it up with the back of a wooden spoon so it cooks evenly. This only takes a few minutes and the chicken should remain pale in colour, not browned.

Take the pan off the heat, then add the dressing mixture to the chicken together with the shallots, kaffir lime leaves, spring onions and three quarters of the ground rice. Mix, then leave to cool for at least 10 minutes so the flavours develop. This dish is served warm or at room temperature, not hot.

To finish, add the herbs, then roughly chop or grind the toasted peanuts and mix half into the chicken. Stir gently. Place the lettuce leaves on a large serving platter and spoon a generous spoonful of the chicken mix over each leaf. Everyone can eat these with their hands so don't overfill them. Garnish with the rest of the ground rice and nuts.

If you prefer, you can serve the chicken with a bowl of sticky rice instead of on lettuce leaves.

Serves 4

500g boneless, skinless chicken (breast or thigh), minced or finely chopped
juice of 1 1/2 limes
4 tbsp uncooked sticky rice
50g unsalted peanuts, roughly chopped
2–3 tbsp vegetable oil
6 Thai shallots, thinly sliced
3 kaffir lime leaves, very finely shredded
3 spring onions, thinly sliced at an angle
30 large mint leaves, roughly chopped
big handful of coriander leaves, roughly chopped
big handful of holy basil, roughly chopped
8–10 baby gem lettuce leaves, small Chinese cabbage leaves or small cos lettuce leaves, washed and drained

Dressing
juice of 1 ½ limes
4 tbsp Thai fish sauce
1 dried chilli, chopped
3 red bird's-eye chillies,
    deseeded and finely chopped
1 ½ tbsp grated palm sugar
1 garlic clove, crushed
10g fresh root ginger, crushed
    and mixed with the garlic

THAI MASSAMAN CHICKEN CURRY

Massaman curry is slightly sweet and fragrant, full of Thai flavour and gentle warmth. It's tasty but it won't blow your head off heat-wise. You'll have enough paste mixture to make two curries so store the rest in the fridge for two or three weeks or pop it in the freezer and keep for up to a month. You can try making this curry with some skinless duck breast too if you like.

Start by making the curry paste. Place a small frying pan over a medium heat, add the cardamom seeds, cumin seeds and cloves and dry roast them for a couple of minutes to release the flavours. Tip them into a small blender or a pestle and mortar and blitz or pound them to make a powder.

Add the remaining ingredients for the paste to the blender or pestle and mortar, plus 2 tablespoons of water, and process or pound to make a smooth paste. Set aside until ready to use.

For the curry, place a medium casserole dish with a lid on a medium heat and add the vegetable oil. Add the onions and cook them slowly for 8–10 minutes until soft and slightly golden. Push the onions to one side of the pan, turn up the heat, then add the chicken strips. Seal them quickly on all sides, without letting them colour too much.

Add half the curry paste and cook for another minute or so, stirring to coat the chicken and the onions with the paste. Add the potato cubes, slashed chillies, stock, coconut milk, chopped tomatoes, lime leaves, palm sugar, soy sauce and 2 tablespoons of the fish sauce. Bring to the boil, put a lid on the casserole dish and reduce the heat to a simmer. Leave to cook for 14–16 minutes or until the chicken is done and no pinkness remains, but take care not to overcook or the chicken will become dry.

Check for seasoning and add a little more fish sauce to taste if needed. Stir in the lime juice and basil, keeping a few leaves for garnish, then add half the chopped peanuts. Spoon the curry into bowls, garnish with the remaining basil, the chopped nuts and some slices of red chilli, then serve with rice.

Serves 4

Chicken curry

2 tbsp vegetable oil

2 red onions, sliced

500g skinless chicken breast cut into 1cm strips

1 large potato, cut into 1cm cubes

2 red bird's-eye chillies, slashed (if you want a hotter curry, add more chillies)

250ml chicken stock

200ml canned coconut milk (low-fat is fine)

2 tomatoes, skinned and roughly chopped

6 kaffir lime leaves

1 ½ tbsp grated palm sugar

2 tbsp soy sauce

3–4 tbsp Thai fish sauce

juice of 1 lime

handful of Thai basil

25g toasted peanuts, roughly chopped

1 large red chilli, deseeded and sliced at an angle

Massaman curry paste

6 cardamom pods, bashed and
   seeds removed (discard the
   husks)
1 tsp cumin seeds
5 cloves
1 ½ star anise
1 tsp white peppercorns
½ tsp ground cinnamon
2 tsp dried chilli flakes
2 tbsp groundnut oil
25g peanuts
5 garlic cloves, roughly chopped
5 lime leaves, finely sliced
30g galangal, peeled and
   roughly chopped
2 lemon grass stalks, white part
   finely chopped
1 tsp Thai shrimp paste
2 tbsp Thai fish sauce
½ tsp grated nutmeg
2 tbsp grated palm sugar

PANANG BEEF CURRY

This recipe shows just how good Thai curries can be if you make your own pastes. Thai cooks make their curry pastes in a big deep pestle and mortar and give the ingredients a good pounding, with what looks like a policeman's truncheon, instead of using a grinding motion. This works a treat. You can also make this with prawns, pork or chicken. Just adjust the cooking times accordingly.

You need a medium-sized casserole dish with a lid. Place the dish on the heat and add the oil. Brown the meat on all sides, working in batches so you don't overcrowd the dish. When all the meat has been browned, tip it back into the casserole dish and add the curry paste (see below). Stir to coat the meat with the paste and cook for 2–3 minutes.

Add the lime leaves, green peppercorns, beef stock and red chillies, then cover and leave to cook gently over a low heat for about 1 hour and 45 minutes. If you prefer, preheat the oven to 140°C/Fan 120°C/Gas 1 and cook the curry in the oven for a couple of hours or until the meat is tender. Have a look every now and then and if the curry looks like it is drying out, add a little water as needed.

When the curry is cooked, stir in the coconut milk, add the tomatoes and red pepper, then continue cooking for a further 10 minutes – the pepper should still have a bit of crunch. Garnish with a sprinkle of fresh coriander leaves and serve with some steamed rice sprinkled with roasted chilli flakes.

Curry paste
Lightly crush the cardamom pods and split them open. Remove the seeds and put them in a spice grinder or a pestle and mortar. You can chuck the pods away.

Heat a small frying pan and dry roast the chillies for 2–3 minutes until slightly browned. Tip them into a small spice grinder or pestle and mortar with the cardamom seeds and return the frying pan to the heat. Add the coriander and cumin seeds to the pan and roast them for a minute to release the flavours, then add them to the cardamom and chillies and grind or pound everything to a powder. Add all the remaining ingredients and pound to make a paste, then set aside. If you prefer, use a spice grinder to blitz the spices to a powder, then transfer this to a food processor, add the remaining ingredients and process to a paste.

There will be enough paste to make 2 curries and you can store it in the fridge for 2–3 weeks or freeze for a month.

Serves 4

2 tbsp vegetable oil
750g lean stewing beef, chopped
   into 1cm cubes
5 lime leaves
2 stems of fresh green
   peppercorns or 1 tbsp sweet
   brined green peppercorns
   from a jar
250ml beef stock
2–3 red bird's-eye chillies, slashed
200ml canned coconut milk
   (low-fat is fine)
3 fresh tomatoes, skinned and
   roughly chopped
1 red pepper, deseeded and cut
   into small dice
fresh coriander leaves,
   to garnish
steamed rice, sprinkled with
   roasted chilli flakes, for serving

Curry paste

6 green cardamom pods,
   seeds only
6 large dried red chillies
1 tbsp coriander seeds
1 ½ tsp cumin seeds
20g galangal, peeled and
   finely chopped
2 lemon grass stalks, white part
   only, finely chopped
4 garlic cloves, roughly
   chopped
10 kaffir lime leaves, finely
   shredded
5 large Thai shallots
   (or 2 banana shallots), roughly
   chopped
2.5cm piece fresh turmeric root,
   finely grated or
   1 ½ tsp ground turmeric
1 tsp shrimp paste
4 tbsp fish sauce
1 tsp salt
1 tbsp vegetable oil

THAI PRAWN NOODLE SALAD

YUM WOON SEN

Glass noodles are very thin noodles, like vermicelli, and they become transparent once cooked. They're also known as cellophane noodles. We love this dish with its fab flavour combo of salty dried shrimp, crunchy peanuts and succulent tiger prawns.

Put the noodles in a large bowl, cover them with just-boiled water and leave for 15 minutes. Drain, then cut the noodles into pieces with scissors so they are easier to eat. Trim the celery and cut it into 2.5cm pieces. Toast the peanuts in a dry pan, then chop them roughly and set aside.

Place a wok over the heat, add 2 tablespoons of oil and gently fry half the shallots until they're golden brown and slightly crispy. Tip them into a large mixing bowl, then add the remaining raw shallots, the chillies, tomatoes, celery, lime juice and fish sauce to the bowl. No need to wash the wok, as you'll need it again.

Add another tablespoon of oil to the wok and fry the dried shrimp for 4–5 minutes, until slightly crispy. Add them to the bowl with the shallots and other ingredients.

Heat 2 tablespoons of oil in the wok and add the sliced garlic. Cook gently until the garlic is just turning light gold, then add the raw tiger prawns. Fry, stirring or tossing them regularly to coat the prawns in the garlicky oil, until they have all turned pink and are cooked through.

Add the prawns to the bowl with the salad, then add the roughly chopped herbs. Toss in the noodles and give the salad a really good mix with your hands. Transfer to a serving dish and garnish with the toasted peanuts.

Serves 4

250g glass noodles
3 sticks of Chinese celery
    or 1 celery stick
40g peanuts
groundnut oil or vegetable oil,
    for frying
20 Thai shallots (or about 8 banana
    shallots), finely sliced
3 red bird's-eye chillies, deseeded
    and finely sliced
12 cherry tomatoes, cut in half
juice of 2 limes
4 tbsp Thai fish sauce
40g dried shrimp
4 large garlic cloves, thinly sliced
500g raw, peeled tiger prawns
    (tails left on), deveined
large handful each of fresh
    coriander, holy basil and mint
    leaves, roughly chopped

THAI JUNGLE CURRY

In the jungle that is the kitchen, preparation is everything! This curry is really quick to cook so get your ingredients prepared and ready to throw into the pan when the time comes. We'll guarantee you'll enjoy making this all the more if you follow our advice. Krachai is a milder version of galangal and ginger – use galangal if you can't get krachai.

Place a large wok on the heat, add the vegetable oil, then add the curry paste (see below). Fry for 3–4 minutes, stirring occasionally. Add the pieces of pork and stir-fry to seal the meat on both sides.

Add the green aubergines, hot stock, chillies and fish sauce. Bring to the boil, then reduce the heat to a simmer and continue to cook for about 5 minutes. Next add the lime leaves, krachai, palm sugar, butternut squash, pea aubergines and fresh green peppercorns. Cook for a further 10 minutes or until the butternut squash and green aubergines are just about done – green aubergines are firmer than the purple ones we usually get in Britain.

Finally add the chopped snake beans and simmer for 4 minutes. Stir both types of basil leaves through the curry and serve with rice.

Jungle curry paste

To make the jungle curry paste, put all the ingredients for the paste in a small blender with 2 tablespoons of water and blitz. Alternatively, finely chop them all, then pound to a paste with the water in a pestle and mortar. It's up to you.

Serves 4

3 tbsp vegetable oil

500g pork tenderloin, cut into thin (5mm) medallions

5 Thai green aubergines, cut into quarters

400g chicken stock, heated

2 red bird's-eye chillies, pierced (see p. 72)

2 tbsp Thai fish sauce

4 kaffir lime leaves

25g krachai, thinly sliced lengthways

1 tbsp palm sugar, grated

400g butternut squash, cut into 1cm cubes

40g pea aubergines

1 stem of fresh green peppercorns or ½ tbsp sweet brined green peppercorns from a jar (optional)

7 snake beans, cut into 2.5cm lengths

handful of holy basil, leaves torn

handful of Thai basil, leaves torn

Jungle curry paste

6 Thai shallots (or 1–2 banana shallots), finely chopped

3 large garlic cloves, finely chopped

25g galangal, peeled and coarsely grated

5 Thai green chillies, deseeded and finely chopped

1 lemon grass stalk, outer leaves removed and white part thinly sliced

6 coriander roots, washed and chopped

½ tsp Thai shrimp paste

3 kaffir lime leaves, finely chopped

1 tsp white peppercorns, crushed

THAI FISH WRAPPED IN BANANA LEAVES

Wrapping fish in banana leaves is a perfect way to retain all the lovely flavours and juices. It's easy to do and when you come to eat it's like opening Neptune's treasure chest. A great dish to cook and enjoy. If you can't get banana leaves, you could wrap your fish in greaseproof paper or foil.

Put all the marinade ingredients in a small blender or a pestle and mortar and blend or pound them to make a paste.

Using a sharp knife, slash the fish 3–4 times through the flesh on both sides. Divide the coriander sprigs, basil leaves and kaffir lime leaves between the fish, placing some in each body cavity.

Run the banana leaves over a gas flame – this makes them pliable. Lay 2 of the banana leaves on the work surface in the form of a cross and place a fish in the centre of the cross. Rub half the marinade into the slashes on each side of the fish. Fold up the banana leaves to make a tight parcel and tie it with string to keep it secure. Repeat with the other fish and the remaining marinade and banana leaves.

Leave the fish to marinate for at least half an hour but the longer the better. You can prepare the parcels well in advance and keep them in the fridge until ready to steam.

Place a large steamer with a lid over a saucepan of boiling water. Put the fish parcels in the steamer, cover with the lid and steam over a gentle heat for 20 minutes. This cooking time works perfectly for 500g fish but if your fish are bigger, allow a little longer. Lovely with a cucumber salad (see page 94) and some rice.

Serves 2

2 x 500g sea bass, scaled and gutted (or other fish such as pomfret or sea bream)
8 sprigs of fresh coriander
12 holy basil leaves
2 kaffir lime leaves
4 banana leaves, about 55cm long

Marinade

4 kaffir lime leaves, finely shredded
2 large garlic cloves, peeled
small handful of coriander leaves and roots
2 Thai shallots, sliced
small handful of holy basil
2 bird's-eye chillies, deseeded and chopped
½ tsp Thai shrimp paste
1 ½ tbsp Thai fish sauce
3 large tbsp coconut cream
juice of 1 lime
15g galangal, peeled and finely chopped or roughly grated

TOKYO

We were blown away by Tokyo. What an amazing city it is –
packed with people, skyscrapers, neon and the most amazing
food. We hadn't known quite what to expect and we found
a whole different attitude to life and cooking here. Quite an
experience!

It had always been our dream to eat sashimi at the Tokyo fish
market and it lived up to our expectations. There was the most
incredible array of fish we'd ever seen in our lives. Everyone
seemed to eat huge quantities of sashimi, more than sushi,
which we didn't see so much of. We did find out lots we didn't
know about sushi though. For example, we learned that you
should never mix wasabi and soy and never dip rice into your
soy sauce. The ginger is a palate cleanser not a relish. The
sight of us piling it on to our sushi caused raised eyebrows in
Japan – it's just not the done thing.

People don't have ovens at home and they rely on the hob,
fish grill and rice steamer to put together quick, healthy and
delicious meals. It's not all raw fish and noodles though. There's
a naughty side to Japanese food and they enjoy lots of deep-
fried dishes. We discovered more about this during a night out
at the yakitori bars when we saw the other side to Japanese
formality and had a rip-roaring night of beer and sing-songs.

Western influence has created a style of fusion food in Japan
called yoshuku. It works really well for us Brits as well as for
the Japanese and by golly it's good. Ingredients like ketchup
and Worcestershire sauce are used alongside trad Japanese
foods to create dishes such as prawn katsu burgers (see page
132). Give them a try and you'll see what we mean.

ASIAN GREENS WITH SESAME SAUCE
CHOI SUM GOMA-AE

Choi sum is a type of green vegetable similar to pak choi. Like all the Asian greens, it's a lovely vibrant colour and makes a great addition to your meal – perfect with miso cod (see page 122). This recipe also works well with spinach or tenderstem broccoli.

Heat a small non-stick frying pan, add the sesame seeds and toast them gently until they've turned lightly golden. Keep a close eye on them so they don't burn. Tip the toasted seeds into a pestle and mortar and pound them until they have nearly turned to a paste but still have some texture.

Add the sugar, soy sauce, dashi and yuzu juice and give it all another good pound to incorporate all the flavours. Sprinkle with a little Japanese pepper – you can use ordinary white pepper if you can't get sansho.

Rinse the greens well, trim the base of the stems and cut the rest into bite-sized pieces.

Put a pan of water on to boil. Put the greens in a steamer and steam over the boiling water for a couple of minutes until tender. Tip them into a warm serving dish and spoon the sauce on top.

Serves 4

6 tbsp sesame seeds
½ tsp sugar
2 tbsp seasoned soy sauce
2 tbsp liquid dashi
2 good splashes of yuzu juice
    or lemon juice
Japanese sansho pepper
600g choi sum (or other greens)

MISO BAKED BLACK COD

After we'd attended a class in Tokyo on how to make our own miso, we decided to impress our teacher with our version of this delectable dish. You can use any good white fish but it should be nice and chunky. Hake steaks would work well. A squeeze of citrus really brings out the flavour so wedges of lime are essential.

Put all the marinade ingredients in a plastic or glass bowl – it must be non-metallic because of the vinegar in the marinade – and mix well. Add the pieces of fish, cover the bowl with cling film and leave in the fridge to marinate for at least 2 hours, but preferably overnight.

When you're ready to cook your fish, preheat the oven to 180°C/Fan 160°C/Gas 4. Lightly oil a non-stick baking tray, then place the fish, skin-side down, on the baking tray. Spoon 2 tablespoons of the marinade over the fish and put the tray in the oven.

Bake for 10–12 minutes, depending on the thickness of your fish. Meanwhile, preheat the grill. Remove the fish from the oven, spoon over the remaining marinade and put the tray under the hot grill until the fish has turned a lovely golden brown.

Serve at once with lime wedges on the side. Great with our Asian greens with a sesame sauce (see page 120).

Serves 4

4 x 200g thick black cod
    fillet, skin on
vegetable oil, for greasing
2 limes, quartered

Marinade
4 tbsp white miso paste
6 tbsp sake
2 garlic cloves, finely grated
10g fresh root ginger, peeled
    and finely grated
2 tbsp caster sugar
1 tbsp seasoned rice vinegar

JAPANESE RICE BALLS
ONIGIRI

You find these little bundles of gorgeousness everywhere in Japan, from service stations to restaurant buffets. They can be filled with anything you fancy, but most popular is salted salmon. This takes at least 24 hours to prepare so if you want an easy option, skip the salted salmon and use ordinary smoked salmon instead. You can also serve the salted salmon in a salad or on its own with some steamed vegetables.

Wash the rice under cold running water until the water runs clear, then cook as the packet instructions. If you have a rice cooker, follow the manufacturer's directions. Leave the rice to cool, but don't put it in the fridge, as it needs to be soft enough to be moulded into the balls.

Have a bowl of cold water at your side so you can wet your hands as you make the onigiri – if your hands are wet the mixture doesn't stick as much. Divide the mixture into 6 and start to shape your rice balls. They don't have to be round. You can be as inventive as you like and form them into cylinders or triangles if you prefer.

Make a dimple in each rice ball and add your chosen filling, such as the salted salmon. Place a small amount of rice over the filling to secure it then reshape the ball – a tidy onigiri is a happy onigiri. Slice the nori sheet into 6 strips and wrap a piece around each rice ball. Sprinkle the onigiri with sesame seeds or dip them into the seeds spread on a plate.

Salted salmon (shiozake)
You'll need a non-metallic container that holds the salmon tightly – a plastic takeaway container might be just the thing. Pour in the sake, then add the salmon, flesh-side down. Cover the container with cling film, then place it in the fridge and leave the salmon to marinate for an hour.

After an hour, remove the salmon and shake off any excess sake. Coat both sides of the salmon evenly with the sea salt, then wrap it loosely in kitchen paper, using plenty of layers. Place the wrapped fish on a plate or into a container and pop it into the fridge for 24 hours. You may leave it as long as 72 hours but the longer you leave it the saltier it will be. Unwrap the salmon and remove any excess salt left on it, then cut into 6 pieces.

Place a non-stick frying pan on a medium heat. Add the pieces of salmon, skin-side down, and cook them for about 5 minutes until the skin is super crispy. Quickly turn the salmon to brown the other side for about 30 seconds each, then transfer the fish to a plate until you're ready to use it.

Makes 6 balls

350g Japanese rice
1 square sheet of nori seaweed
1 tbsp black sesame seeds

Salted salmon
1 tbsp sake
300g salmon fillet, skin on and
    pin-boned
1 1/2 tbsp flaked sea salt

Other filling ideas
tuna and mayonnaise
bonito flakes mixed with soy sauce
pickled radishes
Japanese salty pickled plums
    (umeboshi) – remove the
    stones before putting the
    plums into the rice balls

CHICKEN SHICHIMI KATSU CURRY

Who doesn't love fried chicken? And here it is a with a curry sauce – heaven. Katsu joints are everywhere in Tokyo and katsu dishes are now some of the most familiar Japanese food in Britain. Shichimi is a blend of seven spices and seasonings that's very popular in Japanese cooking. It's a store-cupboard essential and it really brings a dish to life.

Start by making the sauce. Put the coriander seeds, cumin seeds, cardamom pods and fennel seeds in a dry frying pan and heat them gently for a minute or so until lightly toasted – you'll smell their spicy aroma. Keep stirring so they don't burn. Tip the spices into a pestle and mortar or a spice grinder, add the garam masala and pound to form a powder. Remove a teaspoon of the ground spices for coating the chicken and set aside.

Gently heat the vegetable oil in a wok or large frying pan. Add the onion and ginger and cook until soft, then add the remaining ground spices and the tomato purée and stir for a couple of minutes.

Grate the fresh turmeric into the wok or sprinkle in the ground turmeric, if using. Add the coconut milk, chicken stock, sugar and salt, then simmer the sauce for 8 minutes. Remove from the heat and allow the sauce to cool slightly before blitzing it in a food processor or with a stick blender. If the sauce becomes too thick, add a splash of water. Set the sauce aside, ready to reheat later before serving.

Now prepare the chicken. If your chicken breasts are large, and thicker at one end than the other, place them between sheets of cling film and use a rolling pin or meat cleaver to flatten them out a little so they cook evenly.

Beat the eggs in a shallow dish. Put the flour on a second dish, then add the reserved ground spices, then the salt and shichimi seasoning and mix well. Spread the breadcrumbs in a third dish.

Take a chicken breast and dust it in the spiced flour mix. Shake off any excess flour, dip the chicken into the beaten egg and then into the breadcrumbs until evenly covered. Repeat with the remaining chicken breasts.

Pour the oil into a deep non-stick frying pan to a depth of about 1.25cm and heat to about 180°C. Do not allow the oil to overheat and never leave hot oil unattended.

Serves 4

4 x boneless, skinless
  chicken breasts
3 eggs
50g plain flour
1 tsp flaked sea salt
1 tsp shichimi (Japanese
  7-spice seasoning)
100g panko breadcrumbs
  or dry white breadcrumbs
vegetable oil, for shallow frying

Katsu curry sauce

1 ½ tsp coriander seeds
1 tsp cumin seeds
4 green cardamom pods
1 heaped tsp fennel seeds
1 heaped tsp garam masala
2 tbsp vegetable oil
1 medium onion, finely diced
20g fresh root ginger, peeled
  and grated
1 tsp tomato purée
2 x 2.5cm pieces of fresh turmeric
  or 1 ½ tsp of ground turmeric
165ml coconut milk (use low-fat if
  you fancy)
200ml chicken stock
1 tsp sugar
good pinch of flaked sea salt

Once the oil is hot, add the chicken and cook for 4–5 minutes on each side until golden brown and cooked through. Make sure no pinkness remains. Remove and drain on kitchen paper. You will probably only be able to cook a couple of chicken breasts at a time, so keep the first batch warm while you cook the rest.

While the chicken is cooking, reheat the sauce ready to serve. Using a sharp knife, slice the chicken into strips at a slight angle and serve with the Katsu sauce and some steamed Japanese rice.

PORK AND MUSHROOM GYOZAS

Gyozas are Japanese dumplings that are shaped like little Cornish pasties. They're a favourite of ours and the more we cook them, the more we love 'em. We were familiar with the method of making gyoza dough before our trip to Japan but now we've learned some beautiful new fillings. Go gyoza.

First make the dough. Sift the flour into a large bowl and mix in the salt. Stir in the boiling water using a knife or a pair of chopsticks until the mixture comes together. You many not need to use all the water. Roll the dough into a ball, cover with cling film and set it aside to rest for an hour.

Mix the ingredients for the dipping sauce in a small bowl and set aside.

Now for the filling. Drain the mushrooms. Dry the wood ear mushrooms with kitchen paper, slice them into very fine strips, then chop. Squeeze any excess moisture from the shiitake mushrooms with your hands, then cut each mushroom into 3 and slice finely.

Place the pork into a large bowl with the garlic, spring onions and ginger, then add the mushrooms, soy sauce, sake, sesame oil, white pepper, sugar and salt. Now get stuck in and give it all a good mix with your (very clean) hands. Cover with cling film and chill until needed.

Turn the gyoza dough out on to a lightly floured work surface and knead for about 5 minutes until it's smooth and elastic. You can use the dough hook attachment of a food processor for doing this.

Cut the dough into 3 equal pieces and roll each into a ball. Roll out one of the balls on a lightly floured work surface, stretching and turning the dough, until it is as thin as you can make it.

Using a 10cm cookie cutter, cut discs from the gyoza dough and stack them on top of each other, dusting each one with flour before adding the next. Repeat the rolling and cutting process until all the dough has been used.

To assemble the gyozas, hold a disc of dough in the palm of your hand and add a teaspoon of filling mixture – don't be tempted to add more. Using your fingertip, wet the edges of the dough with a little water, then seal the gyoza, pinching it along the edges to create a pleated fan effect. The result should resemble a mini Cornish pasty. Repeat the process until you've used all the filling mixture, setting each gyoza aside on a plate dusted with flour.

Makes 26–28

Dough
300g strong white flour, plus extra
    for rolling and dusting
½ tsp fine salt
200ml just-boiled water

Dipping sauce
50ml black rice vinegar
100ml soy sauce
1 tsp sesame oil

Filling
10g dried wood ear mushrooms,
    soaked in hot water for
    10 minutes
4 dried shiitake mushrooms,
    soaked in hot water for
    10 minutes
300g minced pork
2 garlic cloves, crushed
4 spring onions, cut in half
    lengthways and finely sliced
20g fresh root ginger, peeled
    and finely grated
3 tbsp soy sauce
1 tbsp sake
2 tsp sesame oil, plus extra
    for drizzling
½ tsp ground white pepper
1 tsp caster sugar
1 tsp salt
small bowl of water
vegetable oil, for frying

To cook the gyozas, you need a large frying pan with a lid. Heat a tablespoon of vegetable oil in the pan over a high heat. Add the gyozas to the pan, leaving space between each one – you might need to cook them in batches so you don't overcrowd the pan. Fry them for 2–3 minutes, or until the bottoms are golden brown but take care, as they will burn quickly.

Now add 100ml of water to the pan, cover with the lid and steam the dumplings for a further 2 minutes. Take off the lid and give the pan a shake to release the gyozas from the bottom, then continue to cook for another 2 minutes, until the filling is completely cooked through. Drizzle a little sesame oil around the edges of the frying pan and give it a good shake. Remove the gyozas from the pan and keep them warm while you cook the rest.

Serve the gyozas immediately with the dipping sauce.

SWEET POTATO GYOZAS

Another great gyoza recipe, this one has a lovely veggie filling and it's incredibly economical. These are so delicious that even keen carnivores won't miss meat at all. Make the dough and cook the gyozas as described for the previous recipe.

Preheat the oven to 200°C/Fan 180°C/Gas 6. Put the sweet potato on a baking tray and bake it whole in its skin for 45–60 minutes. Allow it to cool slightly, then scoop out the flesh. Discard the skin, then mash the flesh in a bowl or pass it through a potato ricer. Set aside.

While the potato is baking make the gyoza dough and set it aside to rest (see page 128). Mix all the ingredients for the dipping sauce in a small serving bowl and set it aside.

Once the sweet potato is cold, add the tofu, spring onions, water chestnuts, chilli, miso paste, ginger, garlic, shichimi, salt, white pepper, soy sauce and sesame oil, then mix well. Cut the Chinese cabbage leaves into 4 strips, then shred them finely. Add the cabbage to the mixture with 4 tablespoons of panko breadcrumbs and mix again. If the mixture is slightly sloppy, add another spoonful of panko crumbs. Cover the bowl with cling film and leave to chill in the fridge for 30 minutes to firm up the mixture.

Cut discs of gyoza dough, fill the dumplings and cook as on page 128. Serve the gyozas immediately with the dipping sauce.

Makes 34–35

Dough
300g strong white flour, plus extra for rolling
½ tsp fine salt
200ml just-boiled water

Dipping sauce
½ tsp chilli oil
100ml soy sauce
50ml rice vinegar

Filling
1 sweet potato (about 400g)
125g firm tofu, finely diced
4 spring onions, cut in half lengthways and finely sliced (use three-quarters of the green)
6 water chestnuts, finely chopped
1 large red chilli, deseeded and finely diced
1 tbsp miso paste
20g fresh root ginger, peeled and finely grated
3 garlic cloves, crushed or grated
½ tsp shichimi (Japanese 7-spice seasoning)
1 tsp salt
¼ tsp white pepper
1 tbsp soy sauce
1 tsp sesame oil, plus extra for drizzling
2 Chinese cabbage leaves
4–5 tbsp panko breadcrumbs
vegetable oil, for frying

PRAWN KATSU BURGERS

You'll never turn your nose up at the idea of burgers again after tasting these little marvels. Make them full size or as mini burgers, slider-style, to serve at a party. Posh mini brioche rolls are fantastic for this. The aurora sauce is like a Japanese version of Marie Rose and it's just the ticket with the burgers. And if you don't have any Japanese Worcestershire sauce, good old English is fine.

First make the sauce. Simply mix all the sauce ingredients together in a bowl and set aside until ready to use.

If you have a food processor, add half the prawns to the bowl and pulse them to make a fine paste, then tip this into a mixing bowl. Pulse the remaining prawns until roughly chopped, then add them to the mixing bowl with the rest. Process the onion until finely chopped and add it to the prawns. If you don't have a food processor, chop the prawns and onion as above with a sharp knife.

Add the potato starch or cornflour, plain flour, sake, salt, shichimi, mayonnaise and the 2 egg yolks to the prawns and onion and mix thoroughly. Cover with cling film and leave the mixture in the fridge for at least an hour to chill and firm up.

Divide the mixture into 4 large burgers or 16 small ones. Lightly whisk the egg whites and pour them into a shallow dish. Spread the breadcrumbs in a separate shallow dish.

Heat the vegetable oil to 170°C in a wok or deep-fat fryer. Do not allow the oil to overheat and never leave hot oil unattended.

When the oil is hot add the burgers very carefully. You may need to cook them in batches to avoid overcrowding the pan. A large burger will take 5–6 minutes, turning it occasionally so it cooks evenly, Cook the smaller ones for 2–3 minutes or until golden brown and crispy. Remove the burgers from the pan with a slotted spoon and drain on kitchen paper.

Split the burger buns in half. Put a little tonkatsu sauce on each bottom half, then add a little shredded cabbage and a burger. Top with some aurora sauce and the burger bun lid. If making mini burgers, secure each one with a cocktail stick.

Serve with pots of tonkatsu sauce and aurora sauce so people can help themselves.

**Makes 4 large or
16 mini burgers**

400g raw, peeled prawns,
   deveined
½ medium onion, peeled
1 ½ tbsp potato starch
   or cornflour
1 ½ tbsp plain flour
1 tbsp sake
1 ½ tsp salt
1 tsp shichimi (Japanese-7
   spice seasoning)
1 large tbsp mayonnaise
2 medium eggs, separated
125g panko breadcrumbs
vegetable or groundnut oil,
   for deep-frying
tonkatsu sauce (see recipe
   on p.140 or use ready-made)
Chinese cabbage, shredded
burger buns, brioche rolls,
   or mini rolls

Aurora sauce
4 tbsp mayonnaise
2 tbsp ketchup
2 tsp Japanese mustard
1 tsp Japanese (or English)
   Worcestershire sauce

CHICKEN SKEWERS
YAKITORI

While in Tokyo we went out for yakitori with some salarymen – salarymen are white-collar desk workers who like to let their hair down on a Friday night. We found the yakitori bars in a labyrinth of streets near Shibuya Station in one of the few parts of Tokyo that hasn't yet been gentrified. The streets were full of the smell of charcoal and grilled chicken and our mouths were watering. Out came the sake and the beers and we had a top night. Yakitori are dead simple to make at home, but allow time for marinating the meat. You'll need 12 bamboo skewers too. You can also make yakitori from prawns, pork and offal such as liver and kidneys.

Pour the soy sauce, sake and mirin into a small pan and add the caster sugar, ginger and garlic. Bring to a simmer, stirring constantly until the sugar dissolves, then reduce the heat for a further 5 minutes to cook the garlic and ginger.

Once the garlic is soft, add the rice flour paste to the pan. Bring to a gentle boil, stirring constantly until the sauce has thickened. Strain the sauce through a fine sieve, then pour 125ml of it into a bowl and leave to cool. Put the remaining sauce into a separate bowl and set aside for brushing the yakitori later.

Cut the chicken thighs into bite-sized pieces and add them to the bowl containing the 125ml of cooled sauce. Cover with cling film and leave in the fridge to marinate for at least an hour. Meanwhile, put the bamboo skewers into a shallow dish of cold water to soak for at least half an hour – longer if possible. This will help to stop them burning when on the grill.

Once the chicken has marinated, thread about 4 pieces on to a skewer, alternating them with spring onion. Place the filled skewer on a plate or tray and repeat until you've used all the chicken and spring onions.

Heat a large griddle, barbecue or grill. Place the skewers on or under the grill and cook for about 2 minutes, then turn them and brush the top of the chicken pieces with the sauce. Repeat this turning and brushing about 4 times until the chicken is cooked – this should take about 8 minutes, but always check to make sure it is cooked through and no pinkness remains.

If necessary, you can cook the yakitori in batches and keep them warm in a low oven while you grill the rest. Delicious with rice or on their own. (See the photo on the next page.)

Makes 10–12

500g skinless, boneless
    chicken thighs
8 spring onions, cut into
    5cm pieces

Sauce
100ml soy sauce
50ml sake
75ml mirin
2 tbsp caster sugar
20g fresh root ginger, grated
1 garlic clove, crushed or grated
2 tsp rice flour, mixed with
    1 tbsp water

JAPANESE OCTOPUS BALLS
TAKOYAKI

These are a bit of a passion in Japan and we both enjoyed making and eating them in the Ameyoko street market in Tokyo. You do need to buy a takoyaki pan, but believe us, these octopus balls are simply delicious and well worth the effort for the dedicated foodie. The pans are a bit like steel egg boxes. They're available online and you can get everything from a simple, inexpensive version to a fancy electric number. Turning the balls is a bit of a knack, but don't despair – by ball three we were knocking them out like good 'uns.

Rinse the octopus, then put it into a medium saucepan and add water to cover. Add the dashi and bring to the boil, then turn down the heat and leave the octopus to simmer for about 15-20 minutes or until tender. Strain and leave to cool. Cut the octopus into small pieces – they should be slightly smaller than a sugar cube so they fit into the batter balls.

Make the sauce while the octopus is cooking. Put all the ingredients in a small saucepan and slowly bring to the boil, stirring constantly. Once the sugar has dissolved, turn the heat down to a simmer and cook the sauce for another 5 minutes. Remove from the heat and strain the sauce through a fine sieve into a bowl, then set it aside for later.

To make the batter, put the flour and dashi powder in a mixing bowl, add the eggs and then gradually beat in 275ml of water to make a smooth batter. Leave this to rest for 20 minutes. Add the spring onions and tenkasu (tempura flakes), then pour the batter into a jug.

Heat the takoyaki pan over a gas flame. Once it's hot, add a little groundnut oil to each mould. The oil should be really hot before you add the batter – think Yorkshire puddings. Pour some batter into each mould, filling them nearly to the top and remembering to keep some back for finishing the balls. Reduce the heat and cook the batter until it is firm at the edge but still has a good wobble in the middle. Add a little of the chopped octopus to the centre of each one, pressing it down lightly with the back of a teaspoon. Using a clean teaspoon or a chopstick, carefully turn the ball over and as you do so, add a tiny bit more batter into the bottom of each mould so you have a perfectly round octopus ball once cooked.

When the balls are done, carefully remove them from the moulds and use a pastry brush to coat the balls with the takoyaki sauce. Sprinkle them with bonito flakes and aonori powder, then add a drizzle of mayonnaise. Do your best to leave the balls to cool a little – they will be molten hot inside. Serve with ponzu dressing and some extra takoyaki sauce and enjoy!

Makes 12

500g frozen baby octopus (freezing helps to tenderise it), defrosted and cleaned
50ml liquid dashi
groundnut oil, for frying
bonito flakes
aonori powder
mayonnaise
ponzu dressing, for serving (see p. 154 or buy a jar of ponzu sauce)

Takoyaki sauce
200ml ketchup
25ml soy sauce
25ml mirin
50ml Japanese (or English) Worcestershire sauce
4 large garlic cloves, finely grated
30g fresh root ginger, peeled and finely grated
1 tbsp Japanese pickled ginger, finely chopped
2 tbsp sugar
1 tbsp liquid dashi

Batter

200g plain flour (or okonomiyaki flour)

2 tsp dashi powder

2 large eggs

4 spring onions, finely chopped

35g tenkasu (tempura flakes)

TONKATSU PORK

This is one of those crazy combinations that just works – juicy, deep-fried pork encased in crispy crumbs and served with tonkatsu sauce, which is like a sort of brown barbecue sauce. We cooked this on the riverbank in Tokyo and it is a recipe that we'll make again and again at home.

First make the sauce. Add all the ingredients to a small saucepan and stir well. Bring to a gentle simmer and cook for 5 minutes until the garlic and ginger are both soft and the sauce has thickened slightly – it needs to have a good pouring consistency. When the sauce is ready, strain it through a fine sieve into a bowl, cover with cling film and set aside. The sauce is served at room temperature so don't put it in the fridge.

Now for the pork. Beat the eggs and put them in a shallow dish. Spread the flour in a separate dish and season well with salt and black pepper, then put the breadcrumbs in a third shallow dish.

Take one of the pork steaks, dredge it with seasoned flour, then dip it into the egg and lastly coat with breadcrumbs. Repeat with the remaining steaks and put them on a plate, ready to cook. You can prepare these in advance and leave them in the fridge if you like.

Pour enough oil into a large non-stick frying pan to shallow fry the steaks and place the pan over a medium heat. Add the steaks and fry until golden brown on both sides. They will probably take about 4 minutes on each side but check that they are cooked through before serving. Be careful when turning the steaks so you don't splash hot fat and if necessary, cook the steaks in a couple of batches so you don't overcrowd the pan.

Put the cooked steaks on a serving dish with the shredded cabbage, then drizzle over some sauce. Serve with more sauce on the side and if you want a whole Japanese feast, add some miso soup, rice and Japanese pickles.

Serves 4

2 eggs, beaten
4 tbsp flour
75g panko breadcrumbs
4 thick pork loin steaks
vegetable oil or groundnut oil,
    for frying
½ Chinese cabbage, finely
    shredded
flaked sea salt
freshly ground black pepper

Tonkatsu sauce
125g ketchup (you can get Japanese
    ketchup but any kind will do)
75ml sake
2 tbsp Japanese (or English)
    Worcestershire sauce
2 tbsp dark soy sauce
1 garlic clove, finely grated
1 tsp finely grated fresh root ginger
1 tsp Japanese (or Dijon) mustard
1 tbsp mirin
1 tbsp sugar

SUSHI RICE

Sushi means vinegared rice – it's not a reference to raw fish. Whoever thought of combining this rice with raw fish, pickled ginger and wasabi in all of its wonderful varied forms is a blooming genius. You must have Japanese short-grain rice for making sushi. It's sometimes labelled sushi rice, but any Japanese rice is fine.

First make your sushi vinegar. You can buy this ready-made but it's a doddle to prepare your own. Warm the vinegar in a pan, then add the sugar and salt and let it dissolve. Leave to cool and you have the wonderful sweet savoury dressing for the rice. Set aside.

Wash the rice 3 times, then drain and leave it to stand for 15 minutes. Bring a litre of cold water to the boil and add the kombu (if using) and the rice. Simmer with the lid on for 10 minutes, then leave to stand without taking the lid off for another 20 minutes.

Tip the cooked rice into a large wooden bowl, sprinkle on the sushi vinegar and cut it through the rice with a wooden spatula, using a slicing motion.

Now you need to cool the rice by fanning it for about 10 minutes. You can get a special wooden paddle but we use an old table mat. Turn the rice over and fan for 2 minutes, then repeat this process another 4 times. By this time the rice should be at room temperature and just sticky enough.

Use immediately to make any of the sushi on the following pages, as the rice is past its best after a few hours.

Makes loads

200ml rice vinegar
4 tbsp sugar
4 tsp salt
3cm piece of kombu
    seaweed (optional)
750g Japanese rice

NIGIRI SUSHI

If you like sushi you'll love these recipes which are the stalwarts of the sushi culture. Some are really simple, others more elaborate, but all taste fantastic. Always buy sushi-grade fish, and always make sure it is spanking fresh. Some sushi fish has been deliberately frozen to kill any bacteria.

Carefully cut the fish into strips. Peel the prawns, leaving the tails intact. Butterfly the prawns carefully and remove the dark poop tube. Impale the prawns lengthways on skewers to take out the bend.

Pour 500ml water into a saucepan, add the sake and bring to the boil. When the water is boiling, add the prawns and simmer until pink – this should take about 2 minutes. Remove them from the pan – be careful as the skewers will be hot – and leave to cool. When you take the prawns off the skewers they will be straight, so easier to place on the rice.

Take a ball of rice about the size of a walnut and roll it in your hands to polish the outside. Don't compress the rice too much. Place a dot of wasabi on the top, then put a fish strip or prawn over it. Press it into place with a tapping motion between your thumb and middle finger. Repeat to make as many nigiri sushi as you want, then serve with soy sauce, more wasabi and pickled ginger. (See the photo on the next page.)

selection of fish, such as tuna,
    salmon, brill or sea bass
raw king prawns, shell on
2 tbsp sake
cooked Japanese rice (see p. 142)
wasabi paste
soy sauce and pickled ginger,
    for serving

GUNKANMAKI OR GUNBOAT SUSHI

Shape the rice into balls as for the nigiri sushi above, but make them flatter and shaped like a boat at each end. Cut a strip of nori seaweed about 3cm wide and wrap it around the rice patty, sealing the edge with water. Top with a filling such as salmon roe or a paste made from tuna and mayonnaise, then continue until you've made as many as you want. (See the photo on the next page.)

cooked Japanese rice (see p. 142)
nori seaweed
salmon roe or a mixture of tuna
    and mayonnaise

MAKI ROLLS

You'll need a little bamboo rolling mat for making these little lovelies. They don't cost much and you can get them in major supermarkets and online.

Carefully cut the fish into strips. Peel the prawns, leaving the tails intact. Butterfly them carefully and remove the dark poop tube. Impale the prawns lengthways on skewers to take out the bend.

Pour 500ml water into a saucepan, add the sake and bring to the boil. When the water is boiling, add the prawns and simmer until they're pink – this should take about 2 minutes. Remove them from the pan – be careful as the skewers will be hot – and leave to cool. When you take the prawns off the skewers they will be straight, so easier to handle.

Cover your bamboo rolling mat with cling film. Take half a sheet of nori seaweed and place it on the mat. We think maki rolls made with half a sheet instead of a whole one are tastier, as they are smaller and have a better ratio of filling to rice.

Cover the nori with rice, but leave an empty border of about 2cm on the edge facing you. Press the rice down firmly but gently to give you a thin but even coating. Add strips of fish or prawns down the middle as well as strips of cucumber and avocado – salmon, cucumber and avocado are a good combination, with some wasabi if you like. Roll the mat away from you, catching the filling into the roll. Firm the roll up with the mat.

Remove the mat and using a knife with a damp blade, cut the roll into bite-sized pieces. Serve with soy sauce, pickled ginger and wasabi. (See the photo on the previous page.)

selection of fish, such as tuna, salmon, sea bass or brill
raw king prawns
2 tbsp sake
nori seaweed
cooked Japanese rice (see p. 142)
cucumber
avocado
wasabi
soy sauce, pickled ginger and wasabi, for serving

CALIFORNIA ROLLS

This is an inside-out roll with the rice on the outside and the filling contained by the nori. California rolls are not for the sushi purist but we love them because they are delicious and easy to make.

First place half a sheet of nori seaweed on to the rolling mat. Cover this entirely with rice.

Sprinkle over the toasted black and white sesame seeds. Using the mat, carefully turn this over until the rice is face down on the mat.

Down the middle of the seaweed, lay crabsticks, shredded cucumber, strips of avocado, a line of mayonnaise and finish with some more toasted sesame seeds. Roll it all up firmly, slice and serve. (See the photo on pages 144–145.)

nori seaweed
cooked Japanese rice (see p. 142)
toasted black and white
    sesame seeds
crabsticks
cucumber, shredded
avocado, cut into strips
mayonnaise

RAINBOW ROLLS

The rainbow roll is one of our favourites. It's really like a good helping of sashimi and avocado, wrapped over a California roll. It's got a bit of everything.

Make your California rolls as above but do not slice. Slice the fish into pieces measuring about 5 x 1cm.

Take slices of assorted fish. Near the end of a roll, to your left if you are right- handed, lay a slice of fish over the top, placing it at a 45-degree angle. Close to this, lay 2 parallel strips of avocado. Use the natural shape of the avocado to wrap around the California roll. Repeat using alternate strips of fish and avocado.

Take a sheet of cling film and press the fish and avocado on to the top of the roll, then roll the whole lot up with the rolling mat.

Cut the roll into slices while still wrapped in the cling film, as this keeps it all nice and tidy. Remove the cling film, sprinkle the slices with shichimi seasoning and serve with wasabi, pickled ginger and soy sauce.

California rolls (see above)
tuna, salmon, white fish
avocado
shichimi (Japanese
    7-spice seasoning)
wasabi, pickled ginger and soy
    sauce, for serving

CHICKEN DONBURI

Donburi is actually a term for a bowl, but you'll see the word used for a bowl of rice with other things on top. It's simple to make, beautifully seasoned and comforting – a Japanese one-pot wonder for a family supper.

Cut each chicken thigh into 8 bite-sized pieces. Cut the leek at an angle into slices about 60mm thick and slice the spring onions – also at an angle.

Pour the dashi stock into a wok that has a lid and add the sugar, soy sauce, sake and mirin. Put the lid on the wok and bring everything to the boil. Add the chicken pieces and the slices of leek, then put the lid back on and simmer for 8–10 minutes or until the chicken is just cooked.

Lightly beat the eggs in a small bowl with a pinch of salt and set aside. When the chicken is ready, pour the whisked eggs into the stock and add half the spring onions. Without stirring, let the stock return to the boil, then immediately turn the heat to very low and cover with the lid again. Cook for another 2–3 minutes, until the eggs are set but still soft.

Meanwhile, cook the rice according to the packet instructions and divide it between 4 bowls. Once the eggs are set, spoon the mixture over the rice, then garnish with the remaining spring onions, a sprinkle of Japanese pepper and the shredded nori.

Serves 4

8 boneless, skinless chicken thighs
1 medium leek, trimmed
2 spring onions, trimmed
1.5 litres dashi stock (see p. 156)
1 tsp sugar
2 tbsp soy sauce
1 tbsp sake
1 tbsp mirin
4 eggs, beaten
pinch of salt
300g Japanese rice, for serving
Japanese sansho pepper
1 small sheet of nori, finely
    shredded

TEMPURA SCALLOPS AND ASPARAGUS WITH PONZU DRESSING

We love tempura batter, which is light, crisp and very moreish. Get it right and you have a real treat. Ponzu is a Japanese citrus-based sauce. If you can't get any, use 2 tablespoons of fresh lemon juice and add another 1–2 teaspoons extra to the dressing to taste. The ponzu dressing adds a citrussy zing to this fabulous dish.

For the ponzu dressing, pour the mirin, soy sauce and vinegar into a small saucepan, then add the kombu and bring everything to a simmer. Cook for 3 minutes, or until the liquid is reduced by almost half, stirring occasionally. Remove the pan from the heat and leave to cool.

When the liquid has cooled, remove the kombu and stir in the ponzu sauce or lemon juice. Add a little extra lemon juice if necessary just before serving – you want the dressing to taste very zingy. Pour the dressing into individual dipping bowls and put them on serving plates with slender lemon wedges. Add the spring onion and dried chilli flakes if you like – not strictly authentic but a nice touch.

To make the batter, put the cornflour, self-raising flour and sesame seeds into a large bowl and mix until thoroughly combined. Make a well in the centre. Whisk the egg yolk with half the water in a separate bowl and gradually add this to the flour mixture, using a whisk to draw the dry ingredients into the liquid. When the batter is thick, slowly whisk in the remaining liquid until the batter is just mixed. Don't over-whisk or make the batter too smooth.

Trim the asparagus and cut any particularly long or thick spears in half at an angle. Fill a large saucepan a third full with water and bring the water to the boil over a high heat. Add the asparagus spears, bring the water back to the boil and cook for 1 ½ minutes, or until the spears are just tender. Drain in a colander under running water until cold, then pat dry with kitchen paper and set aside.

Pat the scallops dry on kitchen paper. If using king scallops, cut them in half horizontally through the middle. Leave small queen scallops whole.

Pour oil to a depth of 4cm into a large, wide-based saucepan. Place over a medium heat and heat to 180°C, using a cooking thermometer to check the temperature. Alternatively, use an electric deep-fat fryer. Don't allow the oil to overheat and never leave hot oil unattended.

Serves 6

240g asparagus spears
200–250g queen scallops (without roes) or 18 king scallops (without roes), thawed if frozen
vegetable oil, for deep-frying

Sesame tempura batter

100g cornflour
100g self-raising flour
1 tbsp sesame seeds
1 large egg, yolk only
200ml sparkling water, chilled

Ponzu dressing

100ml mirin
75ml dark soy sauce
1 tbsp rice vinegar
1 x 13cm strip of kombu (dried seaweed)
2 tbsp ponzu sauce (or 2 tbsp lemon juice)
extra lemon juice (optional)
lemon wedges, for garnish
1 spring onion (green part only), finely sliced, (optional)
pinch of dried chilli flakes (optional)

Drop 10–12 of the scallops or scallop pieces into the bowl of batter and turn until lightly coated. Working quickly, take the scallops one at a time with tongs or a couple of forks and drop them gently into the hot oil. Keep the bowl close to your pan, as the batter is thin and will drip off quite quickly. Drop the scallops into different areas of the pan so that they don't get a chance to stick together.

Once all the battered scallop pieces are in the oil, fry for 2–2 ½ minutes, or until pale golden brown and very crisp. Keep an eye on the temperature of the oil so that it doesn't overheat or cool down too much. Use a heatproof slotted spoon to scoop up any bits of the batter that separate from the scallops and to nudge any scallops that stick to the bottom of the pan. They should all float as they fry.

Remove the tempura scallops with the slotted spoon and drain them on kitchen paper. Continue frying the scallops in batches as above until they are all cooked. Add the asparagus to the batter, in batches if necessary, and cook as above for 1 ½–2 minutes, or until crisp. Drain on kitchen paper. Arrange the scallops and asparagus on the serving plates with the ponzu dressing and serve immediately.

DASHI STOCK

This is the basis of many, many Japanese sauces and dressings as well as noodle and soup dishes. Like lots of things in the food world, taking the extra trouble to make your own dashi stock is worth the effort, but you can buy one of the many types of dashi powder, concentrate or liquid. Just follow the instructions on the packet.

Rinse the dried kombu seaweed under cold water.

Pour 1.5 litres of cold water into a large saucepan or stockpot and add the kombu. Leave it to soak for 30 minutes and it will triple in size. Remove the kombu from the pan and cut it into 3 long strips. Put these back in the pan and bring the water to the boil. As soon as the water comes to the boil, remove the kombu and discard. Do not boil the kombu in the water for a long time or the dashi will become bitter.

Stir in the bonito flakes. Bring the water back to the boil and simmer for a couple of minutes, then remove the saucepan from the heat and leave to cool slightly.

Once the bonito flakes have sunk to the bottom of the pan, carefully strain the stock through a sieve lined with muslin or a J-cloth. Allow it to cool and then refrigerate until ready to use. It will keep for a couple of days or can be frozen.

Makes 1.5 litres

10g kombu (dried seaweed), you need a piece about the size of a postcard
1.5 litres water
5g bonito flakes (katsuobushi)

TORIDASHI
PORK AND CHICKEN STOCK

Toridashi is a richer, meaty stock and this is our version which you can make at home – your own Hairy Biker secret recipe. It's great for dishes such as ramen – a good ramen is all about stock.

Preheat the oven to 190°C/Fan 170°C/Gas 5. Put the chicken wings and pork bones in a roasting tin and place them in the preheated oven. Roast for 30–40 minutes until the wings and bones are golden brown, turning them half way through. When they're done, tip the wings and bones in a colander or large sieve and pour a kettle of boiling water over them to remove the excess grease.

While the bones are in the oven, prepare the kombu. Rinse the kombu in cold water, then put it in a large saucepan or stockpot that has a lid, add 2.5 litres of cold water and leave it to soak for 30 minutes.

At the end of the soaking time remove the kombu from the water – it will have tripled in size – and cut it into 3 long strips. Put the kombu back in the pan and bring the water to the boil, then remove it from the heat and discard the kombu. Do not boil the kombu in the water for too long or the stock will be bitter.

Now add the roasted and rinsed wings and pork bones and all the remaining ingredients to the kombu water. Bring everything to the boil, then reduce the heat and put a lid on. Leave the stock to simmer for 2 hours, but don't let it boil or the stock will turn cloudy.

Carefully strain the stock through a sieve lined with muslin or a J-cloth, leaving the bones to drain for 10 minutes. Allow the strained stock to cool, then keep it in the fridge for a day or two or pop it in the freezer.

Makes about 2.5 litres

1.5kg chicken wings
1.5kg pork bones (rib bones are good)
10g kombu (dried seaweed), you need a piece about the size of a postcard
2 thick slices of fresh root ginger
2.5 litres water
250ml sake
1 medium onion, halved
30g bonito flakes (katsuobushi)
6 dried shiitake mushrooms

KYOTO AND RURAL JAPAN

Kyoto is the ancient capital and heart of Japan and it's one of the most beautiful places in the world. The fun started on our journey there from Tokyo, which was a truly great bike ride along motorways with the best service stations ever. We couldn't believe the quality of the food on offer, which is a far cry from what we have at home. It's the tradition in Japan to always take a gift when you go visiting and you can buy great stuff from these service stations. No need to arrive anywhere empty-handed.

We stayed at a monastery outside Kyoto where a Michelin-starred chef cooks for the monks every day. We enjoyed the most amazing breakfast there that was a work of art. There were so many lovely little dishes, all beautifully presented and totally exquisite to eat.

We learned how to make tofu and ramen and how to knead noodles the traditional way – with our feet! We visited an aged noodle maker who showed us how he covered the dough with sheets of plastic and then stomped on it. Back home, we've tried using this method for kneading pasta dough. It works well – and it's good fun. We also discovered the delights of miso soup, which we ate every day for breakfast. It is great stuff and really sets you up for the day.

Japanese food tends to be gentler on the palate than that of some Asian countries but it's always full of flavour. Key ingredients are miso, mirin and soy and there is always a freshness, elegance and style about the dishes. The food is all about balance and harmony and it's good for both your soul and your waistline.

MISO SOUP

The beauty of miso soup is you can add whatever trimmings you like to the broth. The tofu and mushrooms here make a really good veggie option, but fish or raw scallops are good or maybe some duck or sliced pork? You may want to make double this amount because one bowl won't be enough! Although miso has a high salt content it is super healthy, so serve this with a smug I'm-having-miso-soup look on your face.

Pour the stock into a saucepan, add the miso paste and gently bring to a simmer. Add the mirin and soy sauce, then take the pan off the heat.

Now you need 4 bowls for serving and you're ready to pimp your broth.

Cut the mushrooms into quarters and remove the woody end of the stalks. Place a bundle of enoki mushrooms into the bottom of each bowl. Divide the spring onion slices between the bowls and place them neatly with the mushrooms. Cut the tofu into quarters, then each piece into quarters again and place 4 pieces in each bowl.

Place a piece of nori seaweed into each bowl. Pour the hot miso stock over the tofu and vegetables – this will heat the tofu through and cook the mushrooms at the same time. Finally top each bowl of soup with a sprinkling of shichimi, then enjoy. (See the photo on the previous page.)

Serves 4

800ml dashi stock (see p. 156)
4 tbsp white miso paste
1 tsp mirin
1 dsrtsp soy sauce
80g enoki mushrooms
1 spring onion, finely sliced
  at an angle
100g firm tofu
1 small square sheet of nori
  seaweed, divided into 4
a sprinkle of shichimi (Japanese
  7-spice seasoning), to garnish

BEEF SUKIYAKI

This Japanese favourite makes a little beef go a long way. We cooked it with Kobe beef that was tender but eye-wateringly expensive. Fortunately, we reckon that sukiyaki tastes even better with good British beef, which for us has a more beefy flavour, and that's what we use now we're back home. If you like, you can try other types of mushrooms, such as shimeji or oysters.

Cut the beef into thin slices. You want to make them a little thicker than carpaccio slices, more the size of a slice of ham. Top tip from us is to put the beef in the freezer for an hour or 2 to firm up – makes it much easier to slice thinly.

To make the sauce, mix the liquid dashi with 175ml of water in a small bowl or jug, then add the soy sauce and mirin. Set the sauce aside.

Now you need a sauté pan or a large non-stick frying pan with a lid. It's good to have one that's suitable for serving at the table too if you like. Heat the groundnut oil and sesame oil in the pan. Once it's hot, add the beef, then sprinkle it with the sugar, which will help caramelise the meat. Turn the meat over after about 30 seconds – it will cook very quickly as it is so thin.

Push the meat to the sides of the pan. Add all the mushrooms, cabbage, celery, tofu, bamboo shoots and cook for another 2 minutes, just long enough to brown the tofu slightly and wilt the cabbage. Take care not to overcook anything as you want to keep the textures of the ingredients.

Add the sukiyaki sauce to the pan, put the lid on and simmer for 2 minutes. Remove the lid, turn the vegetables and tofu over, then stir the beef into the vegetables and add the spring onions. Simmer for another 2 minutes.

Take the pan to the table so that everyone can help themselves, or serve in bowls with some rice.

Serves 4

450g beef fillet or well-trimmed
    rib-eye
2 tbsp groundnut oil
2 tsp sesame oil
1 ½ tbsp sugar
12 button mushrooms, sliced
4 brown cap mushrooms, sliced
100g enoki mushrooms,
    split into 4
6 fresh shiitake mushrooms,
    cut in half and stalks removed
½ Chinese cabbage, cut into
    2.5cm thick slices
1 ½ celery sticks, sliced at an
    angle into 1.25cm slices
160–175g block of firm tofu,
    cut into cubes
200g bamboo shoots, sliced
    (preferably vacuum-packed,
    but canned will do)
6 spring onions, cut at an angle
    into 3cm pieces
Japanese rice, for serving

Sukiyaki sauce
175ml liquid dashi
150ml soy sauce
50ml mirin

CHICKEN KARAAGE

These are lovely little Japanese chicken nuggets. They're so good and we love them so much we can't stop eating them. They're great on their own with a beer or served up with some rice and veg for a family supper. Easy to make too but don't forget to allow time for the marinating.

Cut the chicken thighs into quarters, making sure that they are all about the same size so they cook evenly.

Put the garlic, ginger, miso paste, soy sauce, sake, shichimi and sugar in a large bowl. Season with a good pinch of salt and mix well. Add the chicken pieces and mix well so they are all thoroughly coated with the mixture. Cover the bowl with cling film and leave the chicken to marinate in the fridge for at least an hour but overnight is even better.

When you're ready to cook the chicken, put the rice flour in a shallow bowl and add a good pinch of salt.

Pour the oil into a large deep saucepan or a wok until it is about a third full – you need enough oil to deep-fry the chicken. Heat the oil to 180°C. Do not allow the oil to overheat and never leave hot oil unattended.

Dip the chicken into the bowl of flour to coat it and place a few pieces in the oil – you'll probably need to fry the chicken in batches so you don't overcrowd the pan. Fry for 4–5 minutes until the chicken is golden and crispy, then drain it on kitchen paper. Keep each batch warm in the oven while you cook the rest, then serve at once with lemon wedges, mayonnaise, and Japanese yellow mustard.

Serves 4

500g boneless, skinless chicken thighs
2 large garlic cloves, grated or crushed
20g fresh root ginger, peeled and grated
1 tbsp miso paste
2 tbsp soy sauce
2 tbsp sake
½ tsp shichimi (Japanese 7-spice seasoning)
1 tsp sugar
175g rice flour
vegetable or groundnut oil, for frying
1 lemon, cut into wedges
mayonnaise and Japanese yellow mustard, for serving
flaked sea salt

MENCHI KATSU BURGER

This is proper Japanese/Western fusion food – a breadcrumbed, fried super-burger served with shredded cabbage and sauce in true tonkatsu fashion. Not a dish for every day but it's no end of a treat when you feel like spoiling yourself. Make these we beg you – they're epic.

Place a small non-stick frying pan over a medium heat and add 2 tablespoons of oil. Once it's hot, add the onion and cook until soft and slightly golden – this will take a good 5 minutes – then set aside to cool.

In a small bowl mix the dashi powder with 2 tablespoons of panko breadcrumbs and the milk.

Put the minced beef and pork in a large bowl and add the Worcestershire sauce, sesame oil, soy sauce, tonkatsu sauce and the egg yolk, then tip in the soaked breadcrumbs and cooled onions. Season well with salt and pepper, then mix everything thoroughly – clean hands are best for this. Divide the mixture into 4 and shape into burgers.

Beat the 2 whole eggs, and pour them into a shallow dish. Spread the flour in a second shallow dish and season with a little salt and the shichimi pepper. Put the remaining 75g of panko breadcrumbs in a third dish.

One at a time, dredge the burgers in seasoned flour, dip them into the egg and then coat with the breadcrumbs. Leave them in the fridge to chill until needed. You can get everything ready in advance if you like and cook them later.

Half fill a large saucepan with oil and heat to 170°C. Do not allow the oil to overheat and never leave hot oil unattended. When the oil is ready, gently put the burgers in and cook for 8–10 minutes until golden and crispy, turning them every couple of minutes. You may need to cook them in 2 batches so you don't overcrowd the pan.

Drain the burgers on kitchen paper, then serve in a burger bun. Add the shredded cabbage drizzled with tonkatsu sauce if you like or serve it on the side. You can also dress your burger with ketchup and/or mayonnaise if you fancy – this is fusion food after all.

For a healthier option, you can cook the burgers in the oven. Preheat the oven to 180°C/Fan 160°C/Gas 4 and lightly grease a non-stick baking tray with oil. Place the burgers on the baking tray, brush them with a little oil and bake for 12 minutes, turning them half way though the cooking time.

Serves 4

vegetable or groundnut oil,
    for frying
1 small onion, finely chopped
1 x 4g packet of dashi stock powder
    (used as a seasoning)
2 tbsp panko breadcrumbs, plus
    75g for coating the burgers
1 tbsp milk
200g minced beef
200g minced pork
1 tsp Japanese (or English)
    Worcestershire sauce
½ tsp sesame oil
2 tsp soy sauce
1 tbsp tonkatsu sauce, plus extra
    for serving
2 eggs, plus 1 egg yolk
3 tbsp plain flour
½ tsp of shichimi pepper
    (Japanese 7-spice seasoning)
4 burger buns (or brioche would
    be nice), toasted
8 Chinese cabbage leaves,
    shredded to garnish
ketchup and/or mayonnaise
flaked sea salt
freshly ground black pepper

MOYASHI BEAN SPROUT SALAD

This is a simple tasty side dish that goes beautifully with recipes such as our panko fishcakes (see page 176). Try to get the soya bean sprouts if you can as they are larger, but ordinary ones will do just as well.

Place the sesame seeds in a dry non-stick pan over a medium heat. Toast them for a few minutes, tossing frequently so they don't stick and burn.

Put 1½ tablespoons of the seeds in a pestle and mortar and pound them to make a paste. Add the chilli oil, soy sauce and vinegar and mix well. Set this dressing aside while you prepare the salad.

Bring a saucepan of water to the boil. Add the bean sprouts and blanch them for 45 seconds, then drain and rinse in ice-cold water. Drain the bean sprouts again and put them in a bowl.

Peel the carrot, slice it in half and cut into fine matchsticks. Cut the celery, leafy top included, into slices, working at a jaunty angle. Mix the carrot and celery with the bean sprouts.

Add the dressing to the salad and toss it through with a couple of forks. Try to lift the vegetables gently so you don't crush them. Top with the remaining sesame seeds and a sprinkle of shichimi seasoning.

Serves 4

2 tbsp sesame seeds
½ tsp chilli oil
2 tbsp seasoned soy sauce
1 tbsp rice vinegar
500g soya bean sprouts or
    ordinary bean sprouts
1 medium to large carrot
1 small celery stick,
    including leaves
shichimi (Japanese
    7-spice seasoning)

JAPANESE PIZZA
OKONOMIYAKI

These are nothing like pizzas really, except that they're round, but that's how they're often described. Okonomiyaki are wonderfully umami, that essence of savoury, and they're fun to make. We went to a special okonomiyaki joint and discovered this great Friday night treat, then we cooked our own and served them up to the Japanese football team after a match. You can buy special okonomiyaki flour online. If you do use this, it contains the yam element of the recipe so leave out the Chinese yam (available in Asian and West Indian stores). You can also buy the okonomiyaki sauce but it's not much effort to make your own.

First make the sauce. Put all the sauce ingredients in a small non-stick saucepan. Gently bring to a simmer, stirring constantly, and cook for 2–3 minutes. Set aside to cool until ready to use.

Into a large mixing bowl put the flour, grated yam (if using), dashi powder and the eggs. Mix thoroughly to form a fairly stiff paste. Add the spring onions and white cabbage, then pour in 70ml of water and mix well to form a thinner paste. Finally add the prawns, bean sprouts and tenkasu and season well with salt and pepper. Fold everything together to coat all the ingredients.

If you have 2 large non-stick frying pans, about 18cm in diameter, you can cook both your okonomiyaki at the same time. If not, cook them one at a time and keep the first okonomiyaki warm in the oven.

Place the pans over a medium heat and add oil to coat the bottom of each. Pour half the mixture into each pan and shape into a neat round which should be about 2cm thick. Cook for about 6–8 minutes until golden brown and slightly set. Lay 6 pieces of bacon on top of each okonomiyaki. Carefully turn the mixture over using 2 fish slices or a couple of pallet knives and cook bacon-side down for a further 4–6 minutes until the batter is cooked through and the bacon is crispy.

Flip the okonomiyaki bacon-side up and brush with the sauce while it's still in the pan. Transfer to plates, bacon-side up, and brush with plenty of okonomiyaki sauce. Sprinkle with the bonito flakes and aonori powder, then add a squeeze of mayonnaise in a wiggly, decorative pattern.

Serves 2

200g plain flour (or okonomiyaki flour, see above)

100g nagaimo (Chinese yam), finely grated

2 tsp dashi powder (used as a seasoning)

3 eggs

4 spring onions, finely sliced

100g small white cabbage, finely shredded

120g raw, peeled tiger prawns, deveined and roughly chopped

100g bean sprouts

25g tenkasu (tempura flakes)

vegetable or groundnut oil

6 rashers of rindless streaky bacon, cut in half

15g bonito flakes

good pinch of aonori (seaweed) powder

mayonnaise

flaked sea salt

freshly ground black pepper

Okonomiyaki sauce
1 tbsp tomato purée
3 tbsp ketchup
4 tbsp liquid dashi
1 tbsp oyster sauce
2 tbsp Japanese
    (or English)
    Worcestershire sauce
1 tsp caster sugar

PANKO FISHCAKES WITH YUZU AND WASABI MAYONNAISE

Everyone loves a good fishcake and this is our Japanese version. We've listed a nicely balanced selection of fish here but feel free to use whatever you fancy. Crisp baby gem lettuce and spring onions tossed in a little olive oil and a splash of yuzu juice go really well with these fishcakes.

Preheat the oven to 180°C/Fan 160°C/Gas 4. Put the potatoes on a baking sheet and bake them for about 1 ½ hours or until cooked through. Leave the potatoes to cool slightly and then remove the flesh and discard the skins. Pass the flesh through a potato ricer for superfine mash or use a normal masher. Once the mash is smooth set it aside to cool completely.

Mix all the ingredients for the dressing in a small bowl, then cover with cling film and leave it in the fridge until needed.

Skin the fish and remove any bones and pin bones. Finely dice all the flesh and put it in a large bowl. Add the prawns, sliced spring onions, edamame beans, Japanese pepper, salt, yuzu juice and sesame oil and mix well.

Once the mashed potato is cold, add it to the fish and mix everything together thoroughly – clean hands are best for this. Divide the mixture into 6 and shape into fishcakes.

Lightly beat the eggs and pour them into a shallow dish. Spread the breadcrumbs in another shallow dish. Dip each fishcake into the egg, then the breadcrumbs and then repeat. This 'double dipping' gives the fishcakes a great crispy coating.

Heat a large deep frying pan, then add vegetable oil to a depth of about 1cm and heat to about 170°C. Shallow fry the fishcakes until crispy and nicely golden on the bottom, then turn them very carefully and cook until the other side is beautifully crisp and golden too. If necessary, cook the fishcakes in 2 batches and keep the first batch warm in a low oven while you cook the rest.

Serve with a good dollop of yuzu and wasabi mayonnaise dressing.

Makes 6 large fishcakes

2 baking potatoes (about 350g each)
150g salmon
150g monkfish
150g tuna
150g cod
150g raw, peeled king prawns, deveined and roughly chopped
4 spring onions, finely sliced
125g shelled edamame beans (frozen are fine but defrost before using)
1 tsp Japanese sansho pepper
2 tsp salt
1 tbsp yuzu juice
1 tsp sesame oil
3 eggs
150g panko breadcrumbs
vegetable oil, for frying

Yuzu and wasabi mayonnaise dressing

8 tbsp mayonnaise
3 tbsp yuzu juice
3 tsp wasabi paste (reduce if you don't like too much heat)
2 tsp sesame seeds

CHASHU PORK

Scoring the pork skin helps the flavours to penetrate so do this yourself or ask your butcher to score it for you. You don't get crackling with this dish but you do get gorgeously sticky, juicy pork. We couldn't stop picking at it. Enjoy the pork by itself or use it to make the delicious ramen on the following page. You could also add the meat to a donburi (see page 150).

Preheat the oven to 140°C/Fan 120°C/Gas 1. Put the soy sauce, sake, mirin, oyster sauce and sugar into a small pan and bring it to a simmer to dissolve the sugar. Place the pork in a small deep roasting tin, then pour the contents of the saucepan over the meat. Add the leek or onion, garlic and ginger to the roasting tin, then pour in 400-500ml of hot water, depending on the width of the tin. Lightly cover the roasting tin with a double layer of foil and place it in the oven. Cook the pork for 2–2 ½ hours, turning it occasionally.

Remove the pork from the oven and leave it to cool in the cooking juices. Once cool, transfer the pork and juices to a sealed container and put it in the fridge until needed. It is easier to carve when fridge cold but if you want to use it sooner, leave it to rest for 20 minutes.

Serves 4

175ml dark soy sauce
120ml sake
3 tbsp mirin
3 tbsp oyster sauce or
    teriyaki sauce
75g sugar
500g belly pork, skin on
    and rolled
½ leek or 1 small onion, sliced
4 garlic cloves, peeled
30g fresh root ginger, peeled
    and thickly sliced
400-500ml hot water

CHASHU PORK RAMAN

Ramen is one of the mainstays of Japanese cooking. It's eaten everywhere and every day in different forms and with various ingredients, but it's always comforting, nutritious and full of flavour and texture. And as if that wasn't enough, it's also flaming great to look at. Ramen is more than a soup – it's a culture and it's catching on more and more in the UK.

Cook the noodles according to the instructions on the packet. Toss the noodles in a little sesame oil to stop them sticking, then keep them warm.

Pour the stock into a saucepan, add the ginger, garlic, shiitake mushrooms and carrot, then bring everything to a simmer for 8 minutes to infuse all the flavours. Add the shimeji mushrooms and cook for a further 2 minutes.

Take 4 large serving bowls and place 4 slices of pork in each bowl. Divide the warm noodles, bean sprouts, bamboo shoots, enoki mushrooms and choi sum between the bowls and arrange them carefully. Pour the hot stock over the pork and vegetables. The heat from the stock will cook the vegetables and reheat the noodles.

Cut the eggs in half and add them to each bowl, together with the spring onions and sliced chilli. Drizzle on a little chilli oil and add a sprinkle of shichimi pepper, then serve right away. Delicious!

Serves 4

750g thick udon noodles
sesame oil
2.5 litres toridashi stock
(see p. 157)
30g fresh root ginger, peeled
and cut into 4 thick slices
2 garlic cloves, cut into slivers.
10 fresh shiitake mushrooms,
cut into slivers
1 carrot, peeled and cut into
matchsticks
100g shimeji mushrooms
16 good slices of chashu pork
(see p. 180)
200g soya bean sprouts
(or ordinary bean sprouts)
50g bamboo shoots, sliced
100g enoki mushrooms
200 choi sum, ends trimmed
and cut in half
4 whole tomago eggs, halved
(see p. 184)
4 spring onions, sliced at an angle
1 long red or green chilli, deseeded
and finely sliced at an angle
chilli oil
shichimi (Japanese 7-spice
seasoning)

MARINATED SOFT-BOILED EGGS
TOMAGO

If you're a fan of pickled eggs, you'll love these, which are just as tasty but not as sharp. Enjoy them as a snack with a beer or use them in the ramen dish on page 182. You'll need a piece of muslin or a J-cloth and remember that the eggs need to marinate for at least 12 hours.

Fill a medium saucepan three-quarters full with just-boiled water and place it on the heat. Once the water has come back to the boil, carefully add the eggs and boil them for exactly 6 minutes. Use a timer, as you want the eggs to be perfect, with lovely runny yolks.

When the eggs are ready, quickly cool them in ice-cold water to stop them cooking. Peel them carefully – remember that they are soft-boiled so they need to be handled gently. Place them in a small container in which they fit snugly.

To make the marinade, pour 100ml of water into a small saucepan and add the soy sauce, mirin, sake and sugar. Gently bring to a simmer and cook until the sugar has dissolved, then remove the pan from heat and leave to cool.

Pour the cooled marinade over the eggs – it should nearly cover them. Place a small piece of muslin or half a J-cloth over the eggs to help make sure they stay covered and get an even coating of marinade. Leave them in the fridge for at least 12 hours, but 24 hours is better, before serving or adding them to your ramen.

Makes 6

6 eggs
100ml light soy sauce
100ml mirin
100ml sake
6 tbsp caster sugar

TOFU MUSHROOM RAMEN

We cooked this in Kyoto, capital of tofu and prayer. It's a great veggie dish but you can also add a steamed chicken breast, cut 1cm thick, instead of or as well as the tofu. If using chicken, you could make the ramen with toridashi stock (see page 157).

Cook the udon noodles according to the instructions on the packet. Once they're cooked, toss them with a little sesame oil to stop them from sticking, then set them aside to keep warm. Peel the carrot and cut it into slices about 2mm thick – carve the slices into pretty shapes if you're feeling fancy. Set the slices aside.

Pour the dashi stock into a medium saucepan and add the sugar, soy sauce, sake, garlic, ginger, shiitake mushrooms and carrot. Bring to the boil, then reduce the heat to a simmer and leave the stock to cook gently while you prepare the rest of the ingredients.

Toast the sesame seeds in a dry non-stick pan, watching them carefully so they don't burn. Beat the eggs and pour them into a shallow dish. Spread the cornflour on a separate dish and the mixed, toasted sesame seeds on a third. To coat the tofu, dip both sides in the cornflour, then the egg and lastly the sesame seeds.

Heat a medium-sized frying pan and add the vegetable and sesame oil. Fry the sesame-coated tofu, turning the slices until golden on both sides, then remove and drain on kitchen paper. Set aside in a warm place.

Take 4 suitable deep serving bowls and place a sheet of nori in each one. Divide the mangetout, pak choi, bean sprouts, oyster mushrooms, enoki mushrooms and the warm noodles between the bowls, arranging them neatly. Pour the hot stock into the bowls – it will cook the vegetables but they should still be crunchy. Top each serving with a piece of hot tofu and half a tomago egg, then garnish with spring onions, chilli, and a sprinkle of schichimi. Finish with a drizzle of chilli oil.

Serves 4

400g udon noodles
(sanuki udon work well)
sesame oil
1 carrot
1.5 litres dashi stock (see p. 156)
1 tbsp sugar
6 tbsp soy sauce
4 tbsp sake
2 garlic cloves, cut into slivers
30g fresh root ginger, peeled and cut
into 4 thick slices
12 shiitake mushrooms, soaked for
30 minutes in just-boiled water
1 heaped tsp white sesame seeds
1 tbsp black sesame seeds
2 eggs
2 tbsp cornflour
175g block of firm tofu, cut into
4 thick slices
3 tbsp vegetable or groundnut oil
1–2 tbsp sesame oil
4 small sheets of nori seaweed
80g mangetout
4 small pak choi, cut in half
200g bean sprouts
100g small oyster mushrooms
100g enoki mushrooms
2 tomago eggs (see p. 184), halved
6 spring onions, sliced at an angle
1 long red chilli, finely sliced
shichimi (Japanese 7-spice seasoning)
chilli oil

SEAFOOD STEW

YOSENABE

Think of this as a kind of Japanese bouillabaisse, with simple fresh flavours that bring out the best in the seafood. It's traditionally made in a clay pot with a lid – either one large one or individual pots. The pots hold the heat well so the food is cooked quickly and efficiently. You can buy individual clay pots in Japanese supermarkets, but it's fine to use a large, shallow casserole dish with a lid. Try to keep the ingredients as separate as possible.

Pour the stock into a large saucepan and add the soy sauce, mirin and sake. Bring the stock to a simmer, then take the pan off the heat. Drain the shiitake mushrooms, remove their stems and cut them into thin slices.

Place a flame-proof casserole dish in the oven at 120°C/Fan 100°C/ Gas ½ to warm through.

Carefully remove the warm dish from the oven. Neatly arrange the carrot strips, spring onions, Chinese leaves, shiitake and enoki mushrooms in the dish, keeping all the ingredients separate. Carefully pour in the dashi stock, then put the lid on and simmer over a very low heat for 3 minutes.

Remove the lid and add the sea bass and prawns, then put the lid back on and cook for 2 minutes, again over a low heat. Add the clams and squid, replace the lid and cook for another minute or until the clams open. Do your best not to move the fish around once added so you have a beautiful dish to present to your guests. Season with a little chilli oil and shichimi.

If you do have individual clay pots, warm them in the oven and prepare the dish in exactly the same way, dividing the ingredients between the pots and arranging them beautifully. Do take great care when handling the pots.

Serves 4

1 litre dashi stock (see p. 156)

4 tbsp soy sauce

2 tbsp mirin

5 tbsp sake

6 dried shiitake mushrooms, soaked for 30 minutes in just-boiled water

1 carrot, peeled and cut into thin strips

4 spring onions, cut into 4cm slices at an angle

8 Chinese leaves, shredded

100g enoki mushrooms, separated into bunches

4 small sea bass fillets, cut in half

12 medium king prawns, peeled and deveined

12 large clams, scrubbed

8 baby squid, cleaned and scored (see pp. 100-101)

chilli oil

shichimi (Japanese 7-spice seasoning)

TOFU, AUBERGINE AND LOTUS ROOT STEW

We cooked this in Kyoto after we'd spent the night at a monastery and taken part in a meditation session so we were feeling well chilled. It's a fab dish that's a celebration of Kyoto's tofu culture. By the way, Japanese aubergines are longer and thinner than the ones we usually get. If you can't find any, use a normal aubergine and dice it into 2cm cubes. You do need fresh lotus root for the crisps, although you can use canned for the rest of the dish. If you don't have fresh lotus root, make the crisps with sweet potato instead.

Start by preparing the lotus root. Bring a large pan of water to the boil. Peel the lotus root, cut off a third and set it aside. Add the rest of the lotus root to the pan. Turn the heat down and cook the root for 30 minutes at a very gentle simmer. Make sure you cook the root straight after peeling, as it will darken quickly. If preparing it in advance, put the lotus root in water with a little vinegar. Canned root does not need preparing in this way and can be added straight to the stew.

Cut the uncooked piece of lotus root into very thin slices on a mandolin or with a sharp knife and use it to make crisps. Half fill a large saucepan with oil and heat it to 170–180°C. If you don't have a cooking thermometer, check that the oil is hot enough by adding a small cube of bread. It should turn crisp and golden and float to the top in a few seconds. Don't overheat the oil and never leave hot oil unattended.

Fry the lotus root slices in a few batches, cooking each batch for about 5 minutes or until golden brown. Drain them on kitchen paper and season with shichimi and salt.

Sprinkle the rice flour on a plate and dip the pieces of tofu into it to coat them. Pour about 5 tablespoons of vegetable oil into a wok and heat, then fry the tofu until lightly golden and slightly crispy and puffy – this will take about 8 minutes. Drain the tofu on kitchen paper and keep warm. You may need to cook the tofu in batches so you don't overcrowd the pan.

Wipe the wok with a little kitchen paper – no need to wash it – then add 2 tablespoons of sesame oil and 2 tablespoons of vegetable oil and place it on a medium heat. Fry the onion for a few minutes until soft, then add the leeks and cook until soft and just slightly golden. Add the sliced aubergine and cook for a further 6 minutes or until soft, tossing the ingredients in the wok occasionally.

Serves 4

1 lotus root (about 400g)
vegetable oil
shichimi (Japanese 7-spice seasoning) 4 tbsp rice flour or cornflour
375g firm tofu, cut into 2.5cm squares
2 tbsp sesame oil
1 medium onion, finely chopped.
2 medium leeks, trimmed and cut into 1cm diagonal slices.
2 Japanese aubergines, sliced into 2cm discs
4 garlic cloves, finely grated.
30g fresh root ginger
2 heaped tbsp miso paste
150g brown shimeji mushrooms, trimmed
4 tbsp mirin
5 tbsp soy sauce
300ml just-boiled water
flaked sea salt

Add the garlic and ginger and fry again for a further couple of minutes, stirring continuously so the garlic doesn't burn.

Cut the cooked (or canned) lotus root into slices of less than 1cm and add them to the onion and aubergine mixture. Now add the miso paste and fry for a minute, then the shimeji mushrooms, mirin, soy sauce and the just-boiled water. Bring the liquid back to the boil, and carefully fold in the tofu.

Spoon the stew into serving bowls and top with the lotus root crisps.

DRIED SEAWEED SALAD

The dressing for this salad is delish. We like to make extra and store it in the fridge to use on salads. You can buy ready-made ponzu dressing but try making your own from our recipe on page 154.

Mix all the ingredients for the dressing in a small bowl, or put them in a jar and give it a good shake.

Put the sesame seeds in a dry non-stick frying pan and toast them over a gentle heat for a few minutes. Keep tossing them so they don't burn.

Soak the seaweed according to the instructions on the packet, then strain and leave to drain. Put it in a bowl, add half the dressing, toss well, then taste. Add more dressing if needed. Top with the toasted sesame seeds just before serving.

Serves 4 as a side dish

1 x 20g packet of dried seaweed
2 tsp sesame seeds

Dressing
1 ½ tsp white miso paste
1 tsp sesame oil
2 tbsp mirin
1 tbsp seasoned rice vinegar
1 tbsp ponzu dressing (see p. 154)

SESAME TOFU
GOMADOFU

We learned lots about tofu while we were in Kyoto. We were shown how to make this special kind by a Michelin-starred chef, who came into the monastery where we were staying every morning to cook for the monks. It's not a soya bean tofu but a different kind, made with sesame paste. It's slightly denser in texture than soya tofu, but equally, if not more, delicious. Taste this and you'll never say tofu is boring again.

Put the kombu in a small non-stick saucepan (a milk pan is ideal) with the water. Leave it to soak for a good hour, then remove the kombu and discard it, reserving the infused water.

Mix the kuzu with the sake in a small bowl to form a paste. Add the tahini (or neri-goma) to the infused water in the pan, then add the kuzu paste. Place the pan over a low to medium heat and stir constantly with a wooden spoon or spatula. Keep stirring vigorously as the mixture starts to thicken.

Once the mixture has thickened, turn down the heat. Simmer for 10 minutes over a very low heat, stirring constantly, or until the mixture is extremely thick and smooth and comes away from the sides of the pan as you stir.

You'll need a suitable container measuring about 17 x 10cm and about 5cm deep – a takeaway container is perfect. Line it with cling film, then pour in the tofu mixture and gently press it down with the back of a spoon. Leave it to cool, then place in the fridge for at least 3 hours to set.

To serve, carefully tip the tofu on to a plate or board and cut it into 4 pieces with a sharp knife. Dip the knife blade into hot water between cuts.

Serve the tofu in small individual dishes and top with a couple of slices of spring onion, a small amount of wasabi and a good dash of soy sauce.

Serves 4

6cm piece of kombu (dried
    seaweed)
300ml still spring water
50g kuzu starch
2 tbsp sake
80g tahini or neri-goma (Japanese
    sesame paste)
1 spring onion, finely sliced
wasabi and soy sauce, for serving

SALMON TERIYAKI

There's so much good, affordable farmed salmon around and we think it's ideal for a tasty teriyaki. This is simple and quick to make but you do need to allow time for the fish to marinate. Try chicken and pork with this recipe too – there's nothing tacky about our teriyaki.

To make the sauce, put the dashi stock, sake, mirin, sugar, ginger and cornflour mixture in a small saucepan. Stir well and place the pan on a medium heat. Keep stirring until the sauce begins to thicken and then continue to simmer for a couple of minutes. Remove the sauce from the heat and leave to cool completely.

Once the sauce is cold, pour half of it into a shallow, non-metallic dish or a zip and seal plastic bag. Add the salmon pieces and leave them to marinate for at least 2 hours, but preferably overnight.

Preheat the oven to 180°C/Fan 160°C/Gas 4.

Place a large ovenproof, non-stick frying pan over a medium heat and add the oil. When the oil is hot, add the salmon, skin-side up, and fry for about 2 minutes until slightly charred. Turn the salmon skin-side down and brush generously with some of the remaining sauce, then place it in the preheated oven. Bake for about 8–10 minutes until the salmon is just cooked through.

Remove the fish from the oven, drizzle with any sauce that's left and serve immediately with wedges of lime and perhaps some green veg and Japanese rice.

Serves 4

600g salmon fillet, skin on,
    cut into 4 equal pieces
3 tbsp vegetable oil

Teriyaki sauce
6 tbsp dashi stock (see p. 156)
3 tbsp sake
4 tbsp mirin
1 heaped tbsp dark brown sugar
20g fresh root ginger, finely grated
2 tsp cornflour, mixed with 1 tbsp
    cold water
1 lime, cut into quarters, for serving

SOUTH KOREA

We didn't know much about South Korean food when we arrived in the country, but we soon discovered what a bold, bright, fiery cuisine it is. We urge you foodies to pay a visit and you won't be disappointed. The food is highly flavoured and just right for us spice-loving Brits. In fact, we've noticed how many Korean restaurants are opening up in Britain and we think this could be the next big thing.

We sampled bibimbap, a lovely, comforting dish made with leftovers, as well as delights such as Korean dumplings and ribbon beef tartare. We found out about the great barbecue tradition – restaurants where you cook your choice of meat to your taste on a grill at the table and help yourself to a selection of dips and accompaniments. Characteristic ingredients in Korean cooking are gochujang chilli paste, gochugaru chilli powder and and a thick soya bean paste called doenjang.

And then there's kimchi, which is a national obsession. Kimchi is made from fermented vegetables, such as cabbage, mixed with various spices and dried anchovies. It's eaten every single day in Korea, served with everything, used in any kind of dish from pancakes to stew. People make kimchi at home, buy it in shops and even have special kimchi fridges for storing their supplies. Kimchi is the true flavour of Korea.

ARMY STEW

This is a first for us – a Spam recipe. A famous dish in Korea, army stew was born at a time after the Korean War, when local people were starving and a certain restaurant owner was determined to help. She invented this dish using Spam taken from American soldiers' dustbins, then the massive surplus they left behind them, and it's still much loved. It's a fantastic, tasty, home-from-the-pub supper and believe us – it's well worth a try. An entire street in Seoul is crammed with restaurants selling this street food sensation. Go on, have a go… it's real fusion food and once you've tried it we guarantee it will become a guilty pleasure.

Heat the oil in a wok or a large frying pan. Add the slices of Spam and the frankfurters, pork mince and tofu. Fry gently until the meat is starting to take on some colour being careful not to break up the pieces.

Add the garlic, chilli paste and chilli powder and fry for 2 minutes, then add the spring onions, noodles and stock. Simmer gently for 10 minutes, then taste and adjust the seasoning. If the stew looks too dry, pour in a little more stock and it's ready to enjoy!

Serve this from the pan at the table with some rice, if you like, or even a big bowl of chips.

Serves 2

2 tbsp vegetable oil

150g Spam (other luncheon meats are available!), cut into thick slices and halved

150g frankfurter sausages, cut into 2cm pieces

150g pork mince

100g firm tofu, cut into 1cm chunks

8 garlic cloves, crushed

3 tbsp gochujang (Korean red chilli paste)

2 tbsp gochugaru (Korean red chilli powder)

8 spring onions, shredded

handful of glass noodles or rice noodles, soaked as instructions on the packet

500ml chicken or pork stock, plus a little extra if necessary

flaked sea salt

freshly ground black pepper

KOREAN MIXED RICE
BIBIMBAP

Like a kind of Korean version of bubble and squeak, this dish is designed to use up the remains of any side dishes left over from the week. Seasoned with chilli paste and topped with a fried egg, this is what Korean comfort food is all about. Our version contains smoked mackerel, but you could make it as a vegetarian meal, or serve it with barbecued meat.

Pour the rice vinegar into a small bowl. Add the sugar and salt and stir vigorously until the granules have dissolved into the liquid. Tip in the chopped cucumber, and give it a good stir so that it all becomes coated with vinegar. Set this aside while you prepare the rest of the dish.

Cook the rice according to the packet instructions. Meanwhile, put a large saucepan of water on to boil. Throw the bean sprouts into the boiling water and allow them to simmer for 45 seconds. Carefully remove the bean sprouts with a slotted spoon, place them in a colander and cool under cold running water, then tip them into a bowl.

Bring the pan of water to the boil again and add the spinach. Mature spinach will take about 1 minute to blanch but the baby leaf stuff is done in no time. Drain the spinach in a colander and cool immediately under running water. Pick up the bundle of spinach and squeeze it tightly to remove as much excess water as possible, then put it on a chopping board and run a knife through it a few times. Place the roughly chopped spinach in a separate bowl.

Pour a teaspoon of sesame oil into the bean sprouts and mix well. Pour the remaining sesame oil, all the soy sauce and the grated garlic in with the spinach and mix really well. Drain the cucumber from its pickling liquid.

Now assemble the dish. Divide the rice between 2 bowls and arrange the spinach, bean sprouts, flaked mackerel and pickled cucumber on top. Add a large dollop of gochujang. Quickly fry the eggs in vegetable oil and add one to each bowl as the crowning glory. The dish may look beautiful now but the traditional way to eat it is to mix everything together into one big mass – definitely the best method we think!

Serves 2

2 tbsp rice vinegar

1 tsp sugar

½ tsp salt

¼ cucumber, peeled, deseeded and chopped into rough 1cm sticks

70g bean sprouts

175g mature spinach, trimmed and thoroughly washed

2 tsp sesame oil

2 tsp soy sauce

½ garlic clove, peeled and grated

200g long-grain rice

1 smoked mackerel fillet, skinned and flaked

2 heaped tbsp of gochujang (Korean red chilli paste)

2 eggs

vegetable oil, for frying

BELLY PORK WITH SESAME SEED DIP
SAMGYUPSAL

These thin slices of griddled belly pork are a culinary wonder in themselves but add the flavours of South Korea to the meat and you have the most fantastic little snack.

Cut the belly pork into thin slices – about half a centimetre thick. Season them with a little salt and pepper and set aside until ready to griddle.

To make the sauce, crush the 2 garlic cloves into a mixing bowl. Finely slice the spring onions and add them to the bowl with the soya bean paste, chilli paste, sesame seeds, sesame oil and golden syrup. Mix well, then pour the sauce into a small serving bowl and set aside.

Remove the leaves from the baby gem lettuces – you will only need the large ones. Wash and rinse the leaves well and set them out on a large serving platter. Slice the 7 garlic cloves lengthways and set aside.

Heat a large cast-iron griddle or frying pan. Add a small amount of vegetable oil, then wipe off the excess with a little kitchen paper. Add some of the seasoned pork slices to the hot pan, together with some garlic slices and fry until the garlic is golden and crispy and the pork is golden brown on both sides – a couple of minutes on each side should be enough. You will need to cook the pork in a few batches, so as each batch is cooked, place it on a warm plate and cover with some foil to keep warm while you cook the rest.

Cut the pork slices in half and place them on the lettuce leaves. Add some crispy slices of garlic on top.

Put the sauce, salted sesame oil and sliced green chilli into 3 separate bowls. Serve them with the pork and garlic lettuce cups so that everyone can add garnishes as they wish.

Serves 4–6

700g belly pork
4 baby gem lettuces
7 garlic cloves
vegetable oil, for frying
small dipping bowl of sesame oil
    seasoned with a pinch of salt,
    for serving
1 green chilli, thinly sliced,
    for serving
flaked sea salt
freshly ground black pepper

Sauce
2 garlic cloves
2 spring onions
3 tbsp soya bean paste
1 tsp gochujang (Korean red chilli
    paste)
½ tsp sesame seeds
½ tsp sesame oil
¼ tsp golden syrup

KOREAN CHICKEN STEW

This is such a good recipe and we think it will become a regular in your kitchen. It's traditionally made with dried anchovies but to make it a bit easier we suggest you use Korean fish sauce (which is anchovy-based) instead, and it will taste just as good. If you do use the anchovies, you need to remove their livers, which taste bitter. Simply slice the head off at an angle, just behind the gills. You'll see a little black bit, which is the liver, so make sure you remove that too.

Cut the chicken into 20 pieces (on the bone) or ask your butcher to do this for you. Make sure you separate the thighs and drumsticks and cut the thighs into 2 pieces each.

Remove the liver from the anchovies (see above), if using. Pour 400ml of water into a small pan and add the fish sauce or the anchovies. Cut the kombu into 2.5cm squares and add them to the pan. Gently bring the water to the boil, then turn the heat down to a simmer and cook the stock for 2 minutes. Remove the pan from the heat – don't leave the stock to boil or it will become bitter. Once the stock is cool, strain, discard the anchovies (if using) and seaweed and set aside until ready to use.

Pierce the chicken legs with a small sharp knife – this will help the marinade to penetrate deeper. Bring a large saucepan of water to the boil, add the chicken pieces and blanch them for a couple of minutes to remove the excess fat. Drain and rinse in cold water.

Now make the marinade. Put the garlic, ginger, soy sauce, chilli paste, mirin, chilli powder, black pepper and caster sugar in a large mixing bowl. Add the chicken pieces and stir so they are well coated in the marinade. Cover with cling film and leave for at least 20 minutes but the longer the better. Alternatively, you can put all the marinade ingredients in a large zip and seal bag and massage them into the chicken through the bag.

Tip half the onions into a large saucepan with a lid, keeping the rest for later. Place the pan over a low heat and add the marinated chicken, making sure you scrape all the marinade into the pan as well. Add the potatoes – the skin helps keep them from breaking up too much. Then add three quarters of the stock and bring it to the boil. Once the stock is boiling, put the lid on the pan, turn down the heat and simmer for 10 minutes.

After 10 minutes carefully stir the stew and add the carrot and remaining onion. Continue to cook over a gentle heat, stirring occasionally, until the potatoes are tender. Add a little more stock if needed, stirring it in gently so as not to break up the potatoes, then serve in bowls.

Serves 6

1 large whole chicken
6 tbsp Korean fish sauce or
    12g dried anchovies
15g kombu (dried seaweed)
2 medium onions, cut into
    2.5cm dice
550g medium potatoes, unpeeled
    and cut into quarters
1 medium carrot, peeled and sliced

Marinade

6 large garlic cloves, crushed
15g fresh root ginger, peeled
    and grated
3 tbsp soy sauce
2 tbsp gochujang (Korean red chilli
    paste)
2 tbsp mirin
2 tbsp gochugaru (Korean red chilli
    powder)
heaped ¼ tsp cracked black
    pepper
1 tsp golden caster sugar

STIR-FRIED COURGETTES
HOBAK BOKKEUM

A fresh crunchy side dish, this is full of texture, flavour and heat. It's great on its own if you're counting calories, but it's also a good partner for meat dishes such as the bulgogi beef on page 242.

Slice the courgettes lengthways into thin ribbons, using a mandolin, a potato peeler or a very sharp knife. Slice them straight into a colander, then sprinkle with the salt and mix well. Leave the courgettes to drain for about 20 minutes to remove some of their moisture.

Place a wok over a low heat, add the oil and fry the garlic until soft. Don't let it burn. Turn up the heat and add the courgettes and thinly sliced onion, then sprinkle in the dried shrimps. Stir or toss the courgettes in the wok until they are softened but slightly crunchy, then add the spring onions, half the chilli, sesame oil and black sesame seeds and heat through for a further minute.

Pile everything into a serving dish and garnish with the rest of the chilli.

Serves 2–3

2 large courgettes
1 tbsp flaked sea salt
2 tbsp vegetable oil
1 garlic clove, cut into thin slivers
½ small onion, finely sliced
20g dried baby shrimps
2 spring onions, finely shredded
    into 2.5cm strips
1 red chilli, sliced into fine strips
1 tsp sesame oil
sprinkle of black sesame seeds

FIERY OCTOPUS
OJINGEO BOKKEUM

We cooked this dish on a rooftop in Seoul and we invited a Korean pop star to share it with us. We'd have liked PSY to come along as well but we had to make do with our Si! This traditional Korean dish is made with squid or octopus that's stir-fried with spicy red chilli paste. Freezing helps to tenderise octopus so it's a good idea to pop it in the freezer for a day or two, even if you've bought it fresh.

If you buy frozen octopus it will come ready-cleaned. Simply rinse it in cold water, pat dry with kitchen paper, then set aside. If you buy fresh octopus, ask your fishmonger to clean it for you.

To make the spice paste, put all the ingredients in a bowl, mix well and set aside.

Bring a medium saucepan of water to the boil. Add the octopus, bring the water back to the boil and blanch for 1–2 minutes, then drain. Allow the octopus to cool slightly, then remove any dark skin – just pull it away from the flesh. Cut the octopus into quarters or if you have very small octopuses, cut them in half and then into bite-sized pieces.

Place a frying pan or wok over the heat and add the vegetable oil. Fry the sliced onion for a couple of minutes, then add the pieces of octopus and the spice paste and cook for another 2–3 minutes. Add the mushrooms and cook for 2 minutes, then add the spring onions and sesame oil. Stir for about 30 seconds to combine the ingredients.

Sprinkle the sesame seeds over the fiery octopus, then garnish with slices of red chilli and serve.

Serves 4

300g frozen baby octopus, defrosted
1 tbsp vegetable oil
1 small onion, thickly sliced
5 shiitake mushrooms, sliced quite thickly (stalks removed)
2 spring onions, cut in half lengthways
1 tsp sesame oil
sprinkle of sesame seeds
1 small red chilli, thinly sliced at an angle, for serving

Spice paste

10g fresh root ginger, grated
3 garlic cloves, grated or finely chopped
2 tsp gochujang (Korean red chilli paste)
1 ½ tsp soy sauce
2 tsp gochugaru (Korean red chilli powder)
½ tsp golden syrup
1 tsp mirin

QUICK KIMCHI SALAD

Kimchi is Korea's national dish and it is everywhere! It takes a bit of a knack to make it yourself, but we've come up with a great alternative that takes no time and is still a spicy, textural treat. We know our kimchi-quick isn't the real thing but it tastes good so give it a try – and we hope it doesn't offend the people of Korea.

Remove the leaves of the Chinese cabbage and trim the stalks. Cut the large leaves into quarters, medium leaves into 3 pieces and the smaller leaves in half. Leave any very small ones whole – each leaf should be a mouthful. Rinse the leaves in cold water in a colander and shake off the excess water.

Layer the leaves in a large bowl, placing the larger, thicker leaves at the bottom and sprinkling each layer with salt – place the tenderest leaves at the top as they will need the least salting. This process brines the leaves and also draws out excess water. Set aside for 30 minutes, then rinse the cabbage leaves thoroughly and leave to drain.

To make the dressing, mix the rice flour with 100ml of water in a small non-stick pan and stir to make a smooth paste. Put the pan on a low heat and heat slowly, stirring constantly until the mixture is thick and gloopy and the flour is cooked, then take the pan off the heat and leave the mixture to cool.

Put the garlic, ginger, anchovy sauce, chilli powder, fermented shrimp, sesame oil and sugar in a bowl, then add the cooled rice flour paste. Mix well, then set aside until ready to use.

Put the slices of onion in a separate bowl, add cold water and leave to soak for 5 minutes, then drain and set aside. This will make the onion slightly milder.

Peel the white radish and cut it into thin slices, then into matchsticks. Set aside.

When everything is ready, assemble the salad. Shake the cabbage leaves to remove any remaining water and put them in a large serving bowl with the drained onions, the white radish and spring onions and mix together. Add the dressing and then mix again, turning over the leaves so they are well coated with the dressing and everything is well combined. Sprinkle with sesame seeds and slivers of red chilli and serve.

Serves 4

1 medium Chinese cabbage
2 tbsp flaked sea salt

Dressing
2 tsp rice flour
2 garlic cloves, grated
25g fresh root ginger, peeled
    and finely grated
1 ½ tsp Korean anchovy sauce
2 tsp gochugaru (Korean red chilli
    powder)
½ tsp Korean fermented shrimps
1 tsp sesame oil
½ tsp sugar
½ small onion, thinly sliced
40g white radish (daikon), peeled
2 spring onions, cut in half and
    quartered lengthways
½ tsp sesame seeds
slivers of red chilli, to garnish

KOREAN DUMPLINGS
MANDU

These little dumplings can be stuffed with different kinds of meat and vegetables and they're hugely popular in Korea. They are similar to Japanese gyozas – available from Asian food stores – and you can use gyoza wrappers for making them. You can buy these or make your own from our recipe (see page 128).

Place the tofu in a bowl and, using the back of a fork or a potato masher, crush the tofu until it is crumbled into small pieces. Add the pork mince, sliced spring onions, bean sprouts, 2 tablespoons of the soy sauce, the fish sauce, chopped garlic and ginger to the bowl. Add a generous amount of salt and pepper, roll up your sleeves and use your hands to mix all the ingredients together.

When you are ready to make your mandu, place a few gyoza wrappers on a clean surface in front of you – it's best to work in batches so the wrappers don't dry out.

Spoon a heaped teaspoon of the mixture into the middle of each wrapper. Wet your finger and run it around the edge of the wrapper. Gently fold the side closest to you over the mixture to meet the edge furthest from you – it should stick. Pick up the wrapper and use your fingers to lightly press the edges together. Try to remove all the air inside the wrapper. When you become more practised you might want to try to put a pleat on the joined edge, but this is only for decoration. Place your finished parcel to one side and repeat the process with the remaining wrappers and filling.

When you have made all the mandu, heat about a tablespoon of groundnut oil in a non-stick frying pan or a wok that has a lid. You'll need to fry the mandu in batches so you don't overcrowd the pan. When the oil is hot, add a few mandu and fry them for about 1 minute until the base looks crisp and golden. Pour in about 40ml of water and put the lid on the pan immediately. Continue to cook over a high heat for about 3 minutes, adding extra water as needed – the idea is to finish with a dry pan and cooked mandu. This does take a little practice, but by the second batch you will have got the hang of it. Repeat the process with the remaining mandu, until all are cooked.

If you're not sure if the mandu are cooked, break one open and if it is cooked through the pork mince will have turned a grey colour. Mix the remaining soy sauce with the rice vinegar and serve it with your mandu.

Makes about 28

125g fresh tofu (not silken)
125g pork mince
3 spring onions, finely sliced
50g bean sprouts, roughly chopped
6 tbsp soy sauce
1 ½ tbsp fish sauce
2 garlic cloves, peeled and very finely chopped
2cm piece of fresh root ginger, peeled and very finely chopped
24 gyoza wrappers (or see p. 128)
groundnut oil, for frying
2 tbsp rice vinegar
flaked sea salt
freshly ground black pepper

RIBBON BEEF TARTARE

YUKHOE

We prepared this at the Olympic archery training centre in Seoul. They love archery with a passion in Korea and they love the spices and flavours in this recipe too. If you like steak tartare this'll blow your socks off. It's simple, quick and a real treat to eat. Note that this recipe does contain raw quail eggs.

Trim away any sinew from the beef, then slice the meat thinly. Pile up a few slices at a time and cut them into super-thin strips. Place the strips in a large mixing bowl.

Crush the garlic, peel and crush the ginger and crush the onion slices through a garlic press into a bowl. Alternatively, put the garlic, ginger and onion in a pestle and mortar and pound them together, then tip everything into a bowl. Finely chop the spring onion and add it to the bowl, then add the soy sauce, sesame oil, chilli powder and sugar and mix well. Add the thin strips of beef to the bowl and stir with a spoon so that all the beef is thoroughly coated with flavour.

Slice the pear into matchstick strips. Remove the leaves from the lettuces and wash and dry them well, then divide the leaves between 4 serving plates. Place some strips of pear on each leaf, then a portion of beef.

Crack the quail eggs, carefully separating the yolks and whites. Make a well in each portion of beef mixture with the back of a teaspoon and add a quail egg yolk. Sprinkle with sesame seeds and serve at once.

Serves 4

500g beef fillet
4 garlic cloves
15g fresh root ginger
4 slices of onion
4 spring onions
4 tbsp soy sauce
1 ½ tbsp sesame oil
2 tsp gochugaru (Korean
    red chilli powder)
2 tsp sugar
1 Asian (nashi) pear
2 baby gem lettuces
4 quail eggs
white sesame seeds

SPICY SOBA NOODLE
AND SEAWEED SALAD

Healthy buckwheat noodles, wakame seaweed and cucumber all bound together with a spicy Korean dressing makes a healthy, delicious and different supper dish. Grilled mackerel goes well with this, as the spicy flavour of the noodles cuts through the oily fish perfectly, but you could make this a vegetarian special by swapping the mackerel for some tofu. Over to you.

Put the chilli paste, rice vinegar and sesame oil in a large bowl to make a dressing for the salad. Mix thoroughly until all the ingredients are fully blended, then set aside. Cook the soba noodles according the instructions on the packet, then drain and run them under cold water and set aside.

Now for the cucumber – you are aiming for strips that resemble spaghetti so keep this in mind. Trim the ends off the cucumber. Using a peeler, remove a strip of peel from the full length and discard. Now peel a strip of cucumber and continue removing long strips until you reach the seedy core, then stop. You should have 4 or 5 long strips of cucumber. Lay a couple on top of each other and carefully slice the lengths of the cucumber into strips about half a centimetre wide. Slice the remaining lengths in the same way, then turn the cucumber over and remove strips from the other side and slice as before. You should now have a large pile of fresh cucumber 'spaghetti'. Add this to the cooked soba noodles, mix well and set aside.

Preheat your grill to maximum. Lightly oil a sturdy baking tray, place the mackerel fillets skin-side up on the tray and season them with salt. Put them under the preheated grill and cook for 7 minutes without turning. By this time the fish will have cooked through and the skin will be lightly browned and blistered in places.

Quickly put your salad together. Drop the rehydrated wakame into the chilli paste dressing and mix until the seaweed is well coated in the dressing. Spoon half the spicy seaweed over the noodle and cucumber mixture, and mix again to coat everything well.

Divide the dressed noodle salad between 2 plates. Add the remaining seaweed, and a fillet of mackerel, then serve at once.

Serves 2

1 heaped tbsp gochujang (Korean red chilli paste)
3 tsp rice vinegar
300g soba (buckwheat) noodles
1 tsp toasted sesame oil
1 cucumber
oil, for greasing
2 mackerel fillets, skin on, pin-boned
15g dried wakame seaweed, soaked and drained according to the packet instructions
flaked sea salt

WHITE RADISH SALAD
SANGCHAE

White radish, also called daikon or mooli, is very popular in Korea and can be eaten cooked or raw. Just the thing you need to go with the barbecue recipes on pages 238–242.

Thinly slice the white radish, stack the slices in neat piles and cut them into matchstick strips. Put these strips with the onion slices in a colander, sprinkle with sea salt, then leave for 10 minutes to drain – the salt draws off the excess moisture from the vegetables. Tip everything into a large bowl.

Put the anchovy sauce, sesame oil, apple vinegar, shrimps, sugar and chilli powder in a small bowl and stir well to combine. Add this mixture to the bowl of white radish and onion and stir thoroughly to coat everything well. Cut the spring onions in half lengthways, then cut each half into quarters and add to the bowl. Sprinkle with sesame seeds before serving. (See the photo on the next page.)

Serves 4

400g white radish
¼ onion, thinly sliced
1 tsp anchovy sauce
½ tsp sesame oil
½ tsp apple vinegar
¼ tsp fermented shrimps
1 tsp sugar
1 ½ heaped tsp gochugaru
    (Korean red chilli powder)
2 spring onions
½ tsp black sesame seeds
flaked sea salt

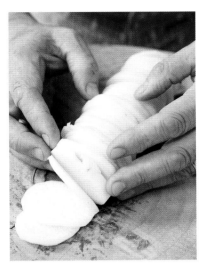

KIMCHI STEW

Kimchi is a kind of fermented vegetable relish, often made with cabbage, that's one of the most popular foods in Korea. In fact, we were told that people say 'kimchi' when they're having their picture taken, just like we say cheese. If you were to conduct a poll of favourite traditional dishes in Korea, then kimchi stew would definitely be up there. Originally cooked to use up kimchi that was starting to 'go over', it has developed into a glorious dish in its own right. Koreans make their own kimchi but you can buy it in Asian food stores.

Heat the oil in a saucepan over a high heat. When the oil is hot, add the chunks of pork belly and fry them until they're lightly browned all over, stirring occasionally.

Drain the kimchi through a sieve, reserving the liquid. Roughly chop the kimchi into 2cm pieces and add them to the saucepan with the pork, then fry for 2 minutes, stirring occasionally.

Scrape in your doenjang and stir to coat all the other ingredients, then pour in 700ml of water and the reserved kimchi juice. Bring to the boil, then turn the heat down and simmer the stew for 10 minutes.

Add the cubed tofu and simmer for another 5 minutes, or longer. Finish the stew with slices of spring onion and serve with bowls of steaming hot rice. This is one of those dishes that can be made and then left on the hob for people to dip into when they want.

Serves 4

1 tbsp groundnut oil
300g pork belly, rind removed,
    chopped into 1cm chunks
200g kimchi
1 heaped tbsp of doenjang
    (soya bean paste) or
    brown miso
250g fresh tofu (not silken),
    chopped into 2cm cubes
3 spring onions, finely sliced
steamed rice, for serving

KIMCHI PANCAKES

Kimchi is more a way of life than a food. Just when you thought there was no other way of preparing kimchi, along come these pancakes filled with the Korean delicacy. We love the addition of crab sticks but you can leave them out if you prefer.

Drain the kimchi through a colander, reserving the drained liquid. Roughly chop the kimchi into small pieces, place these in a bowl, then add the flour and chopped crab sticks.

Measure out 200ml of the reserved kimchi liquid. If you don't have enough, top it up with a little water. Pour the liquid into the bowl with the dry ingredients and crack in the eggs. Using a wooden spoon, beat everything well until you have a smooth batter.

Add about half a tablespoon of oil to a small non-stick frying pan and place over a medium to high heat. When the oil is hot, ladle in about a quarter of the mixture. Leave it to fry, without moving it, for about 2 minutes. Flip the pancake and continue to fry for another 2 minutes. The pancake should be golden on both sides and cooked through. Remove the pancake from the pan and place it on kitchen paper to soak up any excess oil.

Repeat with the remaining batter until you have 4 perfect pancakes. Serve them with a little dish of soy sauce for dipping.

Makes 4 x 15cm pancakes

300g kimchi
200g plain flour
8 crab sticks, roughly chopped
    into 2cm pieces
2 eggs
groundnut oil, for frying
soy sauce, for serving

BULGOGI BEEF

A classic bulgogi beef in Korea is made with blade steak but we tried it with onglet, which works a treat. If you can't get onglet, then sirloin or rump will fit the bill too. If you want to barbecue the meat, leave the steak whole, marinate it in the same way, then place it straight on the grill. Koreans love a barbecue and classic accompaniments are some kimchi (of course!), lettuce leaves, a pot of doenjang (soya bean paste) and maybe some gochujang (Korean red chilli paste).

Place the slices of beef in a bowl and add the garlic, sugar and soy sauce. Get in there with your hands and mix the whole lot together until all the meat is lightly coated with the marinade ingredients. Add the sliced onion and stir with a spoon.

Cover the bowl with cling film, put it in the fridge and leave the meat to marinate for at least 4 hours, but preferably overnight. Take it out of the fridge at least half an hour before you want to cook.

Heat a tablespoon or so of oil in a large frying pan over a high heat until it's smoking. Add the beef and onions, being careful not to overcrowd the pan. You'll probably find it best to cook the beef in a couple of batches. Fry the meat for about 2 minutes without moving it around too much – you want the beef to be just cooked and to have taken on a golden colour in places. Transfer the meat to a plate, garnish with chopped spring onions and serve. (See the photo on the next page.)

Serves 4

600g onglet steak (or sirloin, rump or fillet), finely sliced
2 garlic cloves, finely chopped
1 tsp sugar
4 tbsp soy sauce
1 small onion, peeled and sliced
1–2 tbsp groundnut oil
3 spring onions, green part finely sliced, to garnish

SPICY BARBECUE PORK STEAKS

Korea has a huge barbecue culture. There are loads of great restaurants where you sit at a table with a little grill in the middle and barbecue away to your heart's content, cooking and seasoning your meat just the way you like it. You can cook this beauty under the grill or on the barbecue and it will be great either way. In Korea they often use pork belly but we like these pork leg steaks as an alternative. We've adapted the traditional marinade a little too – and we know you're going to love it.

Place the garlic and ginger in a bowl and add the chilli sauce, soy sauce, rice vinegar and sesame oil. Mix well with a spoon to make a smooth paste with all the ingredients well combined.

Put the pork steaks into a shallow dish and pour over the marinade. Work the marinade all over the meat with your hands or use a spoon and fork. Cover with cling film and leave in the fridge to marinate for at least 4 hours, but preferably overnight.

Remove the marinated meat from the fridge an hour before cooking. Preheat your grill to its highest setting.

Remove the meat from the bowl and lay it on a grill tray. Slide the tray under the grill and cook the meat for about 6 minutes before turning and cooking for a further 6 minutes. The meat should be lightly charred in some places and cooked through.

Leave the steaks to rest for about 5 minutes, then serve them whole, or slice them into smaller pieces. (See the photo on the next page.)

Serves 4

3 garlic cloves, crushed

20g fresh root ginger, peeled and finely chopped

2 large tbsp of gochujang (Korean chilli paste)

2 tbsp soy sauce

2 tbsp rice vinegar

1 tbsp toasted sesame oil

4 thick pork leg steaks, about 225g each

BARBECUE CHICKEN

Another recipe that you can cook under the grill or on a barbecue, but if barbecuing, it's best to use skinless chicken thighs. Be sure to allow plenty of time for marinating the meat. The marinade is really simple to put together but it has a fully formed flavour that works brilliantly with the chicken. And no, we're not shooting our supper here, just learning about Korea's national sport. Korea dominates archery on the world stage and went home with a good clutch of medals after the 2012 Olympics.

Taking one piece of chicken at a time, slash the meat in about 3 places with a sharp knife. Place the chicken in a large bowl.

Add the garlic and ginger to the bowl, pour in the soy sauce and sesame oil, then use your hands to mix the marinade and massage it into the meat. Cover the bowl with cling film and leave the chicken to marinate in the fridge for at least 4 hours or preferably overnight.

Remove the meat from the fridge an hour before cooking. Preheat your grill to its highest setting.

Place the marinated chicken on a grill tray, slide it under the heat and grill the chicken for about 8 minutes on each side. You want the chicken to turn golden and be slightly charred in places and the meat to be cooked through. If you are unsure, cut a chicken thigh open to make sure it is cooked all the way to the bone and that no pinkness remains.

Remove the chicken from the oven and allow it to rest for about 5 minutes before serving. Stack it on a plate and scatter over the finely sliced red chilli, if using. (See the photo on the previous page.)

Serves 4

4 chicken thighs, bone in
    and skin on
4 chicken legs, bone in
    and skin on
5 garlic cloves, crushed
20g fresh root ginger,
    finely chopped
6 tbsp soy sauce
2 tbsp sesame oil
finely sliced red chilli,
    to garnish (optional)

KOREAN RICE CAKE SOUP
TTEOKGUK

This is one of the most comforting of Korean dishes and it's the food Koreans yearn for when they're hung over or have fallen out of love. You do need the Korean rice cakes – there's no real substitute – but you can buy them in Chinese stores and from online suppliers.

Place the rice cakes in a bowl and cover them with water. Leave them to soak for 5 minutes, then drain and set aside.

Beat one of the eggs with a teaspoon of soy sauce and the sesame oil. Heat a tablespoon of the groundnut oil in a small frying pan over a high heat. When it's hot, pour in the egg and cook for about 45 seconds before flipping it over and continuing to cook it for a further 45 seconds. The egg should have puffed up a little and turned golden in places. Slide this mini omelette on to a chopping board, then roll it up and slice into thin 1cm strips. Leave to one side.

Wipe your frying pan clean and pour in the remaining oil. Heat the oil over a high heat, then add the minced beef. Fry the beef for about 2 minutes, breaking up the larger pieces with a wooden spoon, by which time the meat should be cooked through and lightly browned in places. Remove the pan from the heat and pour in the remaining 2 teaspoons of soy sauce. Leave this to one side.

Heat up the stock in a large saucepan. When it's boiling, drop in your soaked and drained rice cakes and boil them for about 1 minute. They are ready when they float to the surface. Meanwhile, crack the remaining 2 eggs into a bowl and whisk.

Reduce the heat so the stock is simmering, then pour in the whisked eggs while stirring the stock with a wooden spoon. Remove the pan from the heat but keep stirring. The eggs will break up into small ribbons.

Divide the soup and rice cakes between 2 bowls. Top each portion with some of the fried omelette and beef. Take the small sheets of seaweed and crush them in your hands, then sprinkle the pieces over the other ingredients. Finish with a final drizzle of sesame oil.

Serves 2 generously

400g Korean rice cakes
3 eggs
3 tsp soy sauce
½ tsp sesame oil, plus extra
    for drizzling
2 tbsp groundnut oil
100g minced beef
1.25 litres light chicken or
    vegetable stock
4 small sheets of roasted
    seaweed (snack-pack size)

KOREAN FRIED CHICKEN

Instead of some KFC, how about some KFC (Korean fried chicken)? This is fab stuff and it's looking like becoming the next big thing in the UK. Remember – you heard about it here first. As you'll see, we've used vodka in this recipe, as we learned that alcohol inhibits the gluten in the flours, making the batter crispier. Traditionally they often double-fry the chicken but no need to do this at home as the batter is so crispy. The addition of fine polenta also helps to make the coating extra crisp. It's really important to have the chicken at room temperature before you fry it, or it won't cook through quickly enough.

Put the garlic and the soy sauce in a bowl. Drop in the chicken thighs and mix well so that the chicken is thoroughly coated, then leave to marinate at room temperature for about 45 minutes.

To make the batter, put the self-raising flour, cornflour, polenta, chilli powder and chilli paste into a bowl, then pour in the vodka and most of the water. Whisk vigorously to make a smooth batter with the consistency of very thick double cream. Add a little more water if needed.

When ready to cook, take each chicken thigh one at a time and lightly coat with flour. Don't go overboard with this, as the soy sauce from the marinade will mix with the flour and turn claggy. It's best just to hold the chicken and dust it with flour.

Heat the oil in a deep saucepan or deep-fat fryer to 170°C. Do not allow the oil to overheat and never leave hot oil unattended.

Cook the chicken in batches so you don't overload your hot oil. Take a few of the floured chicken pieces and dip them in the batter, then carefully lower the chicken into the hot oil. Fry the chicken for about 7 minutes, then place it on kitchen paper to soak up any excess oil. Keep the first batch warm while you cook the rest.

Resist the temptation to dive straight into the chicken – it's best to leave it for at least 2 minutes before eating. Count the seconds as you stare impatiently while salivating – then tuck in.

Serves 4

3 garlic cloves, crushed

4 tbsp soy sauce

8 boneless, skinless chicken thighs

50g self-raising flour, plus a little extra for dusting

50g cornflour

75g fine polenta

1 tbsp gochugaru (Korean red chilli powder)

2 heaped tbsp gochujang (Korean red chilli paste)

75ml vodka

about 150ml water

groundnut oil, for deep-frying

PUDDINGS AND CAKES

We love our puddings but to be honest, we didn't find many sweet dishes that were to our taste on our Asian adventure. That's not to say there aren't loads of good things, but they just didn't seem quite right when we tried to make them back here in Britain.

In this chapter we have included a few authentic favourites, such as a Korean red bean cheesecake, but we've also come up with our own recipes, inspired by wonderful Asian flavours and ingredients such as coconut, mango, passion fruit, pandan leaves and ginger. Some are variations on a familiar theme – meringues flavoured with green tea or crème caramel made with coconut, for example. Others use Asian cooking techniques adapted for a sweet dish – try our Japanese dumplings with sweet soy sauce.

We think these fruity, refreshing little numbers work as well after a Sunday roast as they do after an Asian feast. So instead of apple crumble, enjoy a passion fruit jelly, a lime parfait, or a sake and mint granita. We're sure you're going to love them.

FRIED ICE CREAM WITH BUTTERSCOTCH SAUCE

These are like little warm doughnuts with an ice cream surprise. Not for every day, we know, but what a great treat once in a while. Remember that you need to make the cake-covered ice cream balls the day before you want to eat them, then prepare the sauce on the day.

Line a baking tray with baking parchment. Put the ice cream balls on the tray and then into the freezer for several hours or until the ice cream is hard.

When the ice cream balls are ready to use, put the eggs, cinnamon and orange zest into a small bowl and whisk to combine.

Cut the brioche into 5mm-thick slices. Brush a little of the egg mixture on to one side of each slice of brioche or cake. Wrap each ball of ice cream in brioche, egg side in, totally enclosing the ice cream. Press the covered ice-cream balls in your hand to create an even ball shape and return them to the tray. Put them in the freezer overnight.

To make the butterscotch sauce, put the sugar in a small saucepan with 6 tablespoons of water. Stir the mixture over a low heat, without boiling, until all the sugar has dissolved.

Increase the heat to medium-high and bring the sugar mixture to the boil. Cook without stirring for 10 minutes or until the mixture becomes light golden brown or reaches 165°C on a sugar thermometer. Meanwhile, in a separate saucepan, heat the cream until it is almost boiling.

Remove the syrup from the heat and add the warm cream. The hot mixture may splutter, so do this carefully. Stir until smooth and then strain the sauce into a jug and set it aside to cool. When the sauce is cool, stir in the salt.

Fill a wok one-third full with the oil and place over a high heat. When the surface of the oil is shimmering, add an ice cream ball and cook for a few seconds. Transfer to a serving bowl and repeat with the other ice cream balls. Be careful that the oil doesn't overheat and never leave hot oil unattended.

Serve the fried ice cream immediately, with a drizzle of butterscotch sauce.

Serves 4

8 scoops of good-quality vanilla
    ice cream
2 eggs
1 tsp cinnamon
2 tsp finely grated orange zest
300g brioche loaf or plain
    sponge cake
vegetable oil, for frying

Butterscotch sauce
220g caster sugar
160ml single cream
½ tsp flaked sea salt

FIVE-SPICE POACHED PLUMS

These luscious plums are called five-spice not because they are seasoned with Chinese five-spice powder, but because the recipe includes five different spicy flavourings. It's best to keep the plums whole so when you eat them the flesh falls away in your mouth, bringing a wonderful mixture of tartness, sweetness and spice. Watch out for the stones though – we don't want you breaking your teeth. This is simple and delicious – plum tasty we say – and a good way to use up a glut of fruit.

Rub the vanilla pod between your fingers to soften it, then slice it in half lengthways. Put the pieces in a medium saucepan with the sugar, cinnamon, star anise, peppercorns and ginger, then add 1 litre of water. Bring to the boil and cook for a minute before adding the plums. Reduce the heat to low and simmer for 25–30 minutes, or until the fruit is soft. You may need to weigh the plums down with a sheet of baking parchment and a small lid or plate to keep them submerged in the liquid.

When the plums are ready, remove them with a slotted spoon and transfer them to a serving bowl. Continue to simmer the poaching liquid for a further 25–30 minutes or until it has formed a thick syrup. Pour the syrup over the plums and set them aside to cool.

Serve the plums chilled with some cream and a plate of fortune cookies.

Serves 4

1 vanilla pod
450g caster sugar
1 cinnamon stick
2 star anise
6 black peppercorns
1 tbsp finely grated fresh
    root ginger
12 plums

DOUBLE GINGER ICE CREAM WITH CHOCOLATE SAUCE

Ginger ice cream has a tantalising tropical taste, with the hot spicy flavour of the ginger tempering the richness of the ice cream. We love the luxurious chocolate sauce which is real indulgent naughtiness but so worth it once in a while.

To make the ginger syrup, put the grated ginger and sugar in a small saucepan with 125ml of water and bring to the boil. Swirl the saucepan a little to ensure all the sugar melts, then simmer until the liquid is reduced by half. Remove from the heat and stir in the lemon juice and chopped stem ginger.

To make the ice cream base, put the milk, cream and vanilla pod in a heavy-based saucepan over a medium heat. Bring the milk and cream just to simmering point, then remove the pan from the heat.

Whisk the egg yolks with the sugar until light and foamy. Whisk in a little of the warm milk and cream, then add the remaining liquid, reserving the vanilla pod, and whisk to combine.

Return the mixture to a clean saucepan. Cook over a medium heat, stirring constantly with a wooden spoon, until the mixture thickens and coats the back of the spoon. Strain the mixture into a bowl. Scrape the vanilla seeds from the split pod into the mixture and stir them through. Set the mixture aside to cool before churning in an ice-cream maker, according to manufacturer's instructions.

When the mixture is at the consistency of soft-serve ice cream, spoon in the ginger syrup and complete the churning. Transfer the ice cream to the freezer until you're ready to serve.

To make the chocolate sauce, melt the chocolate in a bowl over a simmering pan of water and then stir in the cream and brandy. Serve the ice cream in scoops with a delectable drizzle of chocolate sauce.

Serves 4

Ginger syrup
2 tbsp finely grated fresh
    root ginger
55g sugar
2 tbsp lemon juice
60g stem ginger in syrup,
    finely chopped

Ice cream base
375ml milk
250ml cream
1 vanilla pod, split lengthways
5 egg yolks
125g caster sugar

Chocolate sauce
100g dark chocolate
150ml single cream
1 tbsp brandy

COCONUT CRÈME CARAMEL

This is a tropical riff on an old favourite. The coconut milk makes a wonderfully creamy crème caramel and papaya or mango are both perfect partners. It's all sensationally sensual on the tongue.

Preheat the oven to 150°C/Fan 130°C/Gas 2. Place 4 x 120ml ramekins in a small deep baking dish.

Melt 115g of the caster sugar with 3 tablespoons of water in a small saucepan over a medium heat, occasionally swirling the sugar in the pan until the sugar has dissolved. Add the cardamom and continue to cook until the syrup has turned a rich dark brown. Remove the pan from the heat and divide the syrup between the ramekins. Tip the ramekins to make sure that the base and sides are well coated with syrup.

Whisk the remaining sugar with the coconut milk, cream and eggs in a bowl until the sugar has completely dissolved. Divide the mixture between the ramekins. Fill the baking dish with enough warm water to come three quarters of the way up the sides of the ramekins.

Carefully transfer the baking dish to the oven and bake for 35-40 minutes or until the custards are set. Remove them from the oven and leave to cool in the baking dish. When cool, cover the ramekins in cling film and refrigerate overnight.

To serve, loosen the crème caramels and turn them out on to plates and serve with sliced papaya or mango.

Serves 4

170g caster sugar
½ tsp ground cardamom
250ml coconut milk
175ml whipping cream
3 eggs
sliced papaya or mango,
   for serving

GOLDEN SPICED JELLY WITH SWEET CHESTNUT AND COCONUT MILK

A separated milk jelly goes Asian. Whether you love or hate milk jelly, try this as it looks great, tastes fantastic and has a clever combo of flavours. The sweetness of the spicy jelly is tempered by the chestnut purée to make a wonderfully sophisticated dessert with a taste of Asia. A jelly for grown-ups.

Put the sugar in a small saucepan with 250ml of water and stir to dissolve. Add the cardamom pods, peppercorns and ginger and bring to the boil. Cook, stirring occasionally, until the syrup turns a toffee colour and the bubbles are getting smaller.

Remove the pan from the heat and leave for a minute, then carefully stir in another 375ml of water. Return the pan to the heat and stir for a minute to ensure all the caramel has dissolved. Then strain the syrup into a measuring jug, discarding the spices, and add enough water to ensure that you have 500ml of liquid. Return this liquid to the saucepan and warm it through.

Meanwhile, soak the gelatine leaves in cold water for about 5 minutes or until they soften. Drain the gelatine and squeeze out the excess water with your hands. Add the gelatine to the warm spice syrup and whisk until thoroughly combined, then leave to cool.

Pour the cooled jelly mixture into 4 glasses or dessert bowls. Cover with cling film and chill in the fridge for several hours or overnight.

Put the chestnut purée, coconut milk and brown sugar in a food processor and process until smooth. Spoon the mixture into a piping bag with a medium-sized star nozzle.

When ready to serve, pipe some chestnut purée on the top of each jelly and then drizzle with some extra coconut milk.

Serves 4

300g caster sugar
6 cardamom pods, crushed
4 peppercorns
2 thick slices of fresh root ginger
4 gelatine leaves
220g unsweetened chestnut purée
80ml coconut milk, plus extra for drizzling
2 tbsp brown sugar

COCONUT AND PANDAN BAVAROIS

Pandan leaves are popular in Asian cooking for their lovely fragrant aroma, which adds sweetness and a pale green hue to desserts. You can also buy pandan essence and paste, both of which can be used for flavouring puddings and cakes.

Toast the coconut in a small non-stick frying pan until it's a lovely golden brown, then set aside. Whip the cream in a bowl, cover with cling film and leave in the fridge until needed.

Pour the milk into a heavy-based saucepan, place over a very low heat and stir in the coconut and sugar. Allow the milk to just simmer for 15 minutes, or until reduced and thick, then strain into a bowl through a fine sieve. Using the back of a large spoon, press as much liquid as possible out of the coconut and into the bowl. Add the pandan essence and green food colouring, if using.

Whisk the egg yolks in a separate bowl, then whisk in the warm milk. Pour the mixture into a clean saucepan and stir over a medium heat for 8–10 minutes, or until the mixture coats the back of the spoon. Pour it into a clean bowl.

Soak the gelatine leaves in a bowl of cold water for 5 minutes, or until softened. Squeeze the excess water from the gelatine leaves and add them to the hot milk and egg mixture. Whisk for a few minutes to ensure the gelatine has completely dissolved. Leave for 45 minutes, or until cool.

Fold the cream through the cooled mixture and spoon into 4 glasses. Cover with cling film and chill for 3 hours or overnight. Just before serving, top with the sliced coconut and passion fruit.

Serves 4

45g desiccated coconut
250ml whipping cream
300ml milk
125g caster sugar
1 tsp pandan essence
2 or 3 drops of green food
    colouring (optional)
4 egg yolks
3 gelatine leaves
sliced fresh coconut and
    passion fruit, for serving

COCONUT CRÊPES WITH BANANAS AND PALM SUGAR

Coconut is hugely popular in South Thailand and we ate loads of beautiful curries and other dishes made with coconut milk. We love crêpes so we thought we'd try making some with a tropical lilt, using coconut milk to create a lovely pud with a taste of Thailand. In our northern heads you can't get any more tropical than banana and coconut – try this and brighten up your next Pancake Day.

Sift the plain flour, rice flour, baking powder and salt into a bowl. Add the sugar, egg and half the coconut milk. Whisk until you have a smooth thick batter, then add the remaining coconut milk and whisk again until combined.

Heat a crêpe pan or a medium-sized non-stick frying pan over a medium heat. Grease it with a little of the butter and then pour in 3–4 tablespoons of batter. Swirl the batter over the base of the pan to form a thin crêpe and cook until golden brown on both sides. Transfer the crêpe to a plate and repeat with the remaining batter until you have 8 crêpes.

Divide the crêpes and sliced bananas between warm plates and sprinkle them with grated palm sugar. Drizzle with some of the remaining coconut milk and serve at once, with lime wedges on the side.

Serves 4

60g plain flour
60g rice flour
1 tsp baking powder
¼ tsp salt
1 tsp caster sugar
1 egg
375ml coconut milk
2 tbsp butter
4 small bananas, halved lengthways
60g palm sugar, grated
4 lime wedges

SAFFRON AND LIME CUSTARD TARTS

These really capture the colour and vibrancy of Asia. You could make these tangy little tarts with kaffir lime juice and zest, but kaffir limes are hard to find in the UK so we've used the ordinary kind. This still makes a lovely little burst of East-West fusion.

To make the pastry, put the flour, sugar and butter in a food processor and pulse until the mixture resembles coarse breadcrumbs. With the motor running, add the beaten egg in a slow but constant stream. Stop processing as soon as the mixture starts to come together. Don't over process. Remove the blade and take out the dough, then shape it into a flattened ball. Roll out the pastry and use it to line 4 x 10cm fluted tart cases. Press the pastry into the sides of the cases and trim. Chill in the fridge for half an hour.

Preheat the oven to 190°C/Fan 170°C/Gas 5. Line the chilled pastry cases with baking parchment and fill with baking beans. Place the tart cases on an oven tray and bake for 10 minutes. Remove the parchment and beans and bake for a further 10 minutes or until the pastry is golden and dry in appearance. Remove the tart cases from the oven and brush the whisked egg white over the cooked pastry. Leave the oven on.

Meanwhile, in a small saucepan bring the cream and saffron almost to simmering point. Remove the pan from the heat and set aside to cool.

Whisk the eggs and sugar until light and creamy and then add the saffron cream and lime juice. Whisk to combine, then stir through the zest.

Divide the mixture between the 4 cases and put them back in the oven. Bake for 12-15 minutes, or until the filling is set but still a little wobbly. Enjoy.

Serves 4

sweet shortcrust pastry (see below or use good-quality shop-bought)
1 egg white, lightly whisked
100ml single cream
a generous pinch of saffron threads
2 whole eggs
80g caster sugar
100ml fresh lime juice
1 tbsp finely grated lime zest

Sweet shortcrust pastry
150g plain flour
1 tbsp caster sugar
100g cold butter, cubed
1 medium egg, beaten

ICED COFFEE PUDDINGS

We noticed that in some places in Asia people drink sweet iced coffee made with evaporated milk so we thought we'd turn this idea into a nifty little sweet. We seem to have forgotten about evaporated milk in this country, but in Asia it is still a popular ingredient. The crispy crumbs make a perfect contrast to the creamy coffee mixture and if you find you have more than you need, they're just the job sprinkled over some ice cream another time. Enjoy these with some of those Japanese chocolate-coated biscuit sticks, known as Pocky biscuits, if you can get them.

Dissolve the coffee in the boiling water and then pour it into a small saucepan and add the evaporated milk and sugar. Warm over a low heat, stirring until the sugar dissolves.

Soak the gelatine in a bowl of cold water for 5 minutes, or until softened. Squeeze the excess water from the leaves and add them to the hot milk mixture. Whisk for a few minutes to make sure that the gelatine has completely dissolved.

When the mixture is cool, pour it into 6 coffee glasses. Cover with cling film and leave them to chill in the fridge for several hours or overnight.

Preheat the oven to 160°C/Fan 140°C/Gas 3. Put the breadcrumbs, brown sugar, cocoa, cinnamon into a bowl, then stir in the melted butter and mix well to coat the crumbs. Scatter the crumbs over a baking tray and bake them in the oven for 10 minutes. Cool and store the crumbs in an airtight container until ready to serve.

To serve, spoon the breadcrumbs over the top of the puddings and serve with chocolate-coated biscuit sticks if you like.

Serves 6

6 tbsp instant coffee or espresso
   powder
120ml boiling water
750ml evaporated milk
80g caster sugar
4 gelatine leaves
60g panko breadcrumbs
2 tbsp brown sugar
2 tbsp good-quality cocoa powder
1 tsp ground cinnamon
80g butter, melted
chocolate-coated biscuit sticks
   (optional)

JAPANESE PEAR DUMPLINGS WITH SWEET SOY DIPPING SAUCE

Nashi pears, also known as Asian pears, are a sort of cross between an apple and a pear and can be eaten raw or cooked. The sweet soy has earthy notes to it which go perfectly with the pear, then add the crispy dumpling and you have a winning combination.

Put the chestnut purée, pear, vanilla bean paste and cinnamon in a food processor or blender and process until smooth. Line a baking tray with baking parchment.

Put a wonton wrapper on a clean surface and brush the edges with water. Put a heaped teaspoon of the chestnut mixture into the centre and then bring the 4 corners of the wonton together. Press the edges as you do so, to seal the mixture inside the wrapper. Place the filled wonton on the lined baking tray and repeat with the remaining wonton wrappers and mixture.

Meanwhile, put the soy sauce, sugar and mirin in a small saucepan and simmer until the brown sugar has dissolved. Set aside to cool.

Fill a wok one third full with the oil and put it over a high heat. When the surface begins to shimmer, carefully lower a dumpling into the hot oil using a slotted spoon. Cook for a few seconds or until the dumpling begins to bubble and expand. Remove it from the heat and drain on kitchen paper. Repeat with all the dumplings, taking care that the oil doesn't overheat. Never leave hot oil unattended.

Dust the warm dumplings with icing sugar and serve them with the sweet soy dipping sauce.

Makes 16

200g unsweetened chestnut purée
1 Asian (nashi) pear, peeled and roughly chopped
½ tsp vanilla bean paste
½ tsp ground cinnamon
16 wonton wrappers
vegetable oil, for deep-frying
icing sugar, for serving

Sweet soy dipping sauce
2 tbsp reduced-salt soy sauce
3 tbsp brown sugar
2 tbsp mirin

PASSION FRUIT JELLY WITH TROPICAL FRUIT

This fabulously fruity jelly is packed with tropical flavours and makes a beautifully refreshing pudding after spicy food. Make the jelly the day before, then add the extra fruit at the last minute. You can use any tropical fruit you like. We love mango and papaya but mangosteens are another favourite of ours and they're available in Asian stores.

Put a fine sieve over a bowl. Slice the passion fruit in half and spoon the flesh into the sieve. Using a spoon, work the seeds into the sieve to extract as much juice as possible – you will need 60ml of passion fruit juice for making the jelly.

Put the orange juice and sugar in a small saucepan with 200ml of water and stir over a medium heat until the sugar has dissolved. Remove from the heat and stir in the passion fruit juice and lime juice.

Meanwhile, soak the gelatine leaves in cold water for about 5 minutes or until they soften. Drain the gelatine and squeeze out the excess water with your hands. Add the gelatine leaves to the warm fruit syrup and whisk until thoroughly combined. Strain the mixture through a sieve if necessary.

Divide the liquid between 4 x 150ml jelly or dariole moulds. Cover them with cling film and leave to chill in the fridge for several hours or overnight until they have set.

Serve the jellies with the papaya wedges and diced fruit and garnish with some extra passion fruit.

Serves 4

8-10 passion fruit, plus extra
    to garnish
300ml fresh orange juice
140g caster sugar
2 tbsp lime juice
6 gelatine leaves
4 wedges of ripe papaya
1 ripe mango, peeled and diced
1 kiwi fruit, peeled and diced

GREEN TEA MERINGUES WITH TROPICAL FRUIT

Green tea is used to flavour lots of Asian sweets and guess what – it's a great idea. We discovered that there are even green tea KitKats so why not green tea meringues? Top this with some tropical fruits and you'll be licking your plate clean.

Preheat the oven to 170°C/Fan 150°C/Gas 3 ½. Line a baking tray with some baking parchment.

Whisk the egg whites with the salt until soft peaks form, then add the sugar, a spoonful at a time. Continue to whisk until the meringue is firm and glossy. Dissolve the green tea powder in the vinegar to make a paste and stir this into the meringue mixture, then whisk in the cornflour.

Drop big spoonfuls of the mixture on to the prepared tray to make 6 individual meringues. Using the back of a spoon, shape the meringues into a nest, making a dip in the centre of each.

Put the meringues in the preheated oven and bake for 5 minutes. Reduce the temperature to 120°C/Fan 100°C/Gas ½ and cook for a further 40 minutes or until the meringues are crisp on the outside. Turn off the oven and leave the meringues to cool in the oven.

To serve, spoon out the flesh from the passion fruit and mix it with the diced fruit. Top each meringue with whipped cream and then spoon over the fruit.

Serves 6

4 egg whites
a pinch of salt
225g caster sugar
3 tsp green tea powder
1 tsp rice vinegar
1 tsp cornflour
6 passion fruit, halved
1 banana, peeled and diced
1 kiwi fruit, peeled and diced
1 mango, peeled and diced
300ml whipped cream

GINGER MOON COOKIES

You'll go nuts for these. Perfect for a Japanese tea ceremony, these ginger cookies are just as good with a big mug of English Breakfast. And for those who dunk, these biccies are dunkable for 2 seconds – if you can wait that long before popping them in your mouth.

Line 2 large baking trays with baking parchment.

Cream the butter and sugar until light and fluffy. Add the ground ginger, vanilla, ground almonds, flours and salt and stir until the dough starts to come together. Add the crystallised ginger and, using your hands, work the ginger evenly into the dough. When the ginger is all worked through, press the dough together to form a flat disc. Wrap the dough in cling film and chill in the fridge for 10 minutes.

Cut the chilled dough in half and roll it out between 2 sheets of baking parchment to a uniform thickness of 3mm. Transfer the dough to the fridge and chill for 15 minutes. Repeat with the second piece of dough.

Preheat the oven to 180°C/Fan 160°C/Gas 4. Cut circles of dough out with a 6cm cookie cutter and place them on the lined baking trays. Bake for 10–12 minutes or until the cookies are golden brown. Remove them from the oven and use the cookie cutter to make a half moon indent in the hot cookies. Leave them to cool for a while on the baking trays, then transfer to wire racks to cool completely.

Store the cookies in an airtight container.

Makes 24

125g unsalted butter
125g dark brown sugar
1 tbsp ground ginger
½ tsp vanilla bean paste
50g ground almonds
75g rice flour
65g plain flour
pinch of salt
70g crystallised ginger,
  finely chopped

CHILLED WATERMELON WITH CHILLI SYRUP

Once you get the chilli habit you just can't get enough of it. Here it is, partnered with super-cool watermelon and nashi pears for a beautifully refreshing sweet treat. Fire and ice – it can be nice.

Put the sugar in a saucepan with 125ml of water and add the chilli flakes, diced chilli and star anise. Bring to the boil and cook until the sugar has dissolved and the mixture has formed a light syrup. Remove from the heat, discard the star anise and stir in the lemon juice. Pour the syrup into a jug and chill until ready to serve.

Core the nashi pears and cut them in half, then cut each half into 4. Cut the chilled watermelon into chunks and serve with the wedges of nashi pear, mint sprigs and a drizzle of chilli syrup.

Serves 4

115g caster sugar
¼ tsp dried chilli flakes
1 large red chilli, deseeded
    and finely diced
1 star anise
2 tbsp lemon juice
2 chilled Asian (nashi) pears
1.5kg chilled watermelon
mint sprigs, for serving

LIME PARFAIT WITH SHATTERED CHILLI TOFFEE

Mmm... this beautifully tangy little parfait is set off to perfection by the crisp chilli toffee. These make an impressive final flourish to any meal.

Put the lime juice and sugar in a small saucepan and bring them to the boil. Boil for 3 minutes until the mixture forms a thick, clear syrup.

Meanwhile, whisk the egg yolks with an electric beater until they have doubled in size, then slowly pour the hot syrup over the yolks, whisking continuously. Continue to whisk until the mixture has cooled. Lightly fold the crème fraiche and lime zest into the mixture, then pour it into 4 dariole moulds. Cover with cling film and freeze overnight or until set.

To make the chilli toffee, line a small baking tray with baking parchment. Put the sugar and chilli flakes into a small saucepan and warm over a low heat until the sugar melts. You may need to swirl the sugar over the base of the saucepan to help it melt, but don't stir it with a spoon. When the sugar has melted completely and has turned a golden-brown toffee colour, remove it from the heat and pour it into the lined baking tray. Tip the tray a little to ensure the toffee coats the tray evenly and thinly. Leave the toffee to set, then break it into shards.

To serve, remove the lime parfaits from the freezer and run a warm knife around the inside of the moulds. Turn them out on to chilled plates and top with shards of the chilli toffee.

Serves 4

100ml lime juice
90g caster sugar
4 egg yolks
300g crème fraiche
2 tbsp finely grated lime zest

Chilli toffee
150g caster sugar
½ tsp dried chilli flakes

PANDAN CHIFFON CAKE

This is popular in Thailand and other parts of Asia and it is no plain Jane of a cake. The pandan leaves really bring it to life and guess what? It's green! Pandan leaves and essence are used in Asian cooking to flavour both sweet and savoury dishes and you can buy them from Asian food stores or online. Freeze any leaves that you have left over and remember to remove the leafy star before eating.

Preheat the oven to 170°C/Fan 150°C/Gas 3 ½. Grease a 22cm springform cake tin and line it with baking parchment.

Take 8 of the pandan leaves and trim off the bottom so they measure about 10–12cm. Arrange them in the base of the cake tin, with the tips pointing outwards to form a star. Chop the remaining leaves and the trimmings, then pop them in a food processor with 50ml of water and blend for 3 minutes or so until puréed.

Strain the purée through a muslin cloth into a bowl. Gather the ends of the cloth and squeeze the pulp gently to release all the juice into the bowl. Add the coconut milk, the pandan essence (if using) and the green food colouring. Set aside.

Separate the eggs, putting the whites in a large super-clean bowl (wipe it with a little lemon juice or vinegar to remove any grease). Whisk the egg whites with the cream of tartar and a pinch of salt until soft peaks form, then gradually add 60g of the caster sugar, a dessertspoon at a time. Keep whisking until the egg whites are glossy and form stiff peaks.

In a separate large bowl, beat the egg yolks with the remaining caster sugar until the mixture is pale in colour. Sift the flour into the sugar and egg yolk mix and fold together. Now gently – and we mean gently – fold in the egg whites a third at a time. Make sure each third is thoroughly incorporated before adding the next.

Pour the mixture into the lined cake tin, taking care not to disturb your beautifully arranged pandan star. Bake in the preheated oven for 40–45 minutes. When the cake is done, leave it to cool for 10 minutes in the tin, then turn it out on to a wire rack to cool completely. Remove the pandan star before eating.

Serves 8–10

8–10 pandan leaves
75ml unsweetened coconut milk
1 tsp pandan essence (optional)
4–5 drops of green food colouring
8 eggs
1 tsp cream of tartar
pinch of salt
135g caster sugar
175g self-raising flour

LYCHEE AND GINGER PAVLOVA

If you like your desserts in the style of Carmen Miranda's hat, this one is for you. A different, but really delicious version of pavlova, this is particularly good with fresh lychees if you can bear peeling them. You can use tinned, but the flavour is not as good. It's best to get everything ready in advance, then put it all together at the last minute and serve at once before the meringue has a chance to go soggy.

Preheat the oven to 180°C/Fan 160°C/Gas 4.

Put the egg whites in a large bowl and start to whisk them with an electric hand whisk. When the whites have increased in volume and are starting to hold their own weight, add a couple of tablespoons of the sugar, and continue to whisk to incorporate. Continue to whisk while gradually adding the rest of the sugar, a little at a time, until all the sugar has been incorporated. Then whisk for a further 2 minutes by which time the whites should be glossy and forming stiff peaks.

Pour the vinegar into a small bowl, add the cornflour and mix well. Pour this mixture into the egg whites, scraping all the remnants from the bowl. Whisk for a further 2 minutes to ensure the cornflour mixture has been thoroughly mixed into the meringue.

Line a flat baking tray with baking parchment. Spoon dollops of the meringue mixture on to the tray and use the back of a spoon to push them out into a circle roughly 25cm in diameter. It doesn't have to be too neat so don't worry.

When you're happy with your meringue place it in the oven and immediately reduce the temperature to 110°C/Fan 90°/Gas ¼. Bake for 1 hour and 10 minutes, then turn the oven off and leave the meringue in the oven for at least 3 hours or even overnight.

To make the cream, place the mascarpone, crushed ginger nuts, double cream and half of the chopped stem ginger into a bowl. Use a wooden spoon to beat the ingredients together to create quite a thick topping. Add a few splashes of milk to loosen the consistency slightly, until it reaches the point of being like very thick whisked cream.

Dollop the mixture on top of the cooked meringue and spread it out with a spoon or knife. Top with the prepared lychees and the rest of the chopped stem ginger. Drizzle the pavlova with some of the stem ginger syrup before scattering with rose petals. Serve at once!

Serves 6

5 egg whites
225g sugar
1 tbsp white malt vinegar
2 tbsp cornflour
150g mascarpone
200g ginger nut biscuits, crushed
300ml double cream
about 5 chunks of stem ginger, chopped into small pieces, plus some of the syrup
milk
24 lychees, peeled and stones removed
rose petals, to garnish

COCONUT AND STICKY RICE PUDDING WITH LIME AND PAPAYA SALAD

From Torquay to Thailand, everyone loves a rice pudding and here is one with a teasingly exotic touch. We cooked this on a tropical island beach – it was paradise. Now we're home, every mouthful brings back wonderful memories so close your eyes and join us.

Soak the rice in 300ml of water for at least 30 minutes or up to 4 hours, even overnight. Drain the rice and wash it thoroughly.

Take a bamboo steamer with a lid and line it with greaseproof paper, a banana leaf or some muslin. If using paper or banana leaf, use a skewer to pierce it with lots of holes. You want plenty of steam to get through, but don't make the holes too large or the rice will fall out.

Pour water into a saucepan that the steamer can sit on or use a wok – the water should be about 5cm deep. Place the rice in the steamer and put on the lid. Bring the water to the boil, then turn down the heat and steam the rice for about 20 minutes or until it is tender.

While the rice is cooking, pour the coconut milk into a small saucepan and add the salt, palm sugar and kaffir lime leaves. Warm the milk through over a medium heat, stirring frequently, for 5–7 minutes so the flavours infuse, but do not allow it to boil.

Cut the papaya in half and remove the seeds, then peel the flesh and cut it into neat slices. Divide the slices between 4 plates or arrange them on a serving dish and add the zest and juice of the limes and the mint sprigs.

Once the rice is cooked, put it in a mixing bowl and gradually add three quarters of the infused coconut milk, a quarter at a time. Keep the final quarter for finishing the pudding. Mix well and leave to cool for 10-15 minutes. Drizzle over the remaining coconut milk at the last minute and serve with the papaya.

Serves 6

200g Thai sticky rice
1 x 400ml can of coconut milk
¼ tsp salt
50g palm sugar, roughly chopped
5 kaffir lime leaves

Papaya salad
1 ripe papaya
juice and zest of 2 limes
4 mint sprigs, to garnish

RED BEAN CHEESECAKE

Here's a cheesecake with a difference. Sweetened red beans are often used in desserts in Korea and Japan and this is a winner. The red bean flavour is subtle but delicious. Note that the recipe contains raw eggs.

Line a 22cm springform cake tin with greaseproof paper. Roughly break the biscuits into a food processor, then, with the machine running, pour in the melted butter. Tip the mixture, which should resemble light rubble, into the base of the cake tin and use the back of a spoon to spread the biscuits evenly over the base. Put the tin in the fridge while you get on with the rest of the recipe.

Put the egg whites in a clean bowl and whisk until light, frothy and holding their shape. While continuing to whisk, pour in a third of the sugar and whisk until well incorporated, add another third while continuing to whisk – the eggs should be turning glossy and stiff by now. Pour in the final third of the sugar and whisk until you have a stiff meringue. Keep this to one side.

In another bowl, beat together the cream cheese and the crème fraiche until well combined. Put the gelatine leaves in a bowl of cold water and leave them to soak for 5 minutes.

Pour the milk into a pan and warm it over a gentle heat until it is about blood temperature. Remove the gelatine from the water and squeeze out as much excess water as you can. With the pan still on the heat, gradually stir the gelatine into the warm milk but do not let the milk boil. When the gelatine has fully dissolved, scrape the mixture into the mixed cream cheese and crème fraiche, and beat again to incorporate.

Use a spatula to dollop half of the meringue into the cream cheese mix. Beat the mixture with a spatula until well mixed before dropping in the remaining meringue. Mix this meringue in more gently, making sure it is fully incorporated but keeping a light touch.

Purée the red beans in a food processor or blender, then add them to the mixture, folding them in until smooth. Pour the mixture into the prepared tin and flatten the surface as neatly as you can. Place the cheesecake in the fridge for at least 6 hours, but preferably overnight.

When ready to eat, carefully remove your cheesecake from the tin and peel off the greaseproof. Grate over some chocolate or add chocolate curls for a final flourish before serving up your very Korean cheesecake.

Serves 8–10

250g digestive biscuits
80g butter, melted
3 egg whites
90g sugar
250g cream cheese (such as Philadelphia)
250g crème fraiche
3 gelatine leaves
50ml milk
400g canned sweetened red beans (azuki beans)
grated chocolate or chocolate curls, to garnish

SAKE AND MINT GRANITA

Look at this – purer than a spring on Mount Fuji! The granita can be made with soju, a Korean alcoholic drink, but we like it with sake. It's easy to put together but needs to be left to freeze overnight, so make this the day before you want to serve it.

Put the sugar in a saucepan with 500ml of water and place it over a high heat. Bring the mixture to the boil, stirring more frequently as it heats up. As the liquid comes to the boil, take the pan off the heat, and stir again to make sure the sugar has fully dissolved.

Add the mint leaves and grated ginger, then leave the mixture to infuse for 20 minutes. Strain it through a sieve, pour in the sake and lime juice, then stir well so that everything is thoroughly mixed. Leave to cool to room temperature.

Pour the mixture into a plastic or metal container and put it in the freezer. Leave it for about an hour, by which time there should be ice crystals forming around the edges of the granita. Using a fork, scrape these from the sides and mix them into the liquid centre, then put the granita back in the freezer. Check the granita every 35 minutes or so, scraping the ice crystals and mixing as before. When the mixture has all turned to ice crystals, cover the container with a lid or cling film and leave to freeze overnight.

When ready to serve, scoop the granita into cold glasses and garnish with a little lime zest and a few extra mint leaves.

Serves 4-6

180g sugar
20g mint leaves, plus a few extra
    to garnish
20g fresh root ginger, grated
350ml dry sake (14%)
juice and zest of 1 lime

INGREDIENTS A-Z

Here are some of the ingredients used in recipes in this book that you might not be familiar with. Many are available in supermarkets and the rest can be found in Asian stores and from online suppliers (see our list on pages 306–308).

Apple aubergines

Apple aubergines are round and may be green, yellow, orange or purple in colour. They have a clean, crisp flavour and can be eaten raw or cooked. They are available in Asian stores and some supermarkets.

Banana leaves

These big bendy leaves are used for wrapping food in Thai cuisine, infusing the contents with their sweet, subtle flavour. They also make an attractive background for serving food – like disposable plates! Buy them fresh or frozen.

Bird's-eye chillies

These small chillies are extremely hot! They are sometimes called Thai chillies, and ripen from green to orange, then red.

Black rice vinegar

Black rice vinegar is dark in colour and is made with black glutinous rice. It has a smoky sweetness that is perfect with noodles, soups and dumplings.

Bonito flakes

These brown, smoky flakes are also known as *katsuobushi*. They are made of dried, smoked skipjack tuna, which is shaved into thin flakes. They are used to make dashi stock, but can be added as a topping or seasoning to many savoury dishes.

Chilli oil

This spicy oil has a real kick to it, and is known as *rayu* or *layu* in Japan. Pinkish in colour, it is typically a chilli-infused sesame oil. Use it to add a touch of fire to any savoury dish, or mix it with soy sauce and rice vinegar to make a dip.

Chinese cabbage

Chinese cabbage has pale, tightly wrapped leaves and thick white ribs. Its mild, sweet flavour can be used in stir-fries, salads and stews.

Chinese 5-spice powder

An essential seasoning for much Chinese cooking, this spice mix is made up of five key ingredients: star anise, cinnamon, cloves, Sichuan pepper and fennel seeds. Its pungent flavour is a tasty balance of sweet and savoury. Add a small pinch to marinades and rubs, or stir-fries and rice for a hint of warmth and flavour.

Chinese sausages (or lap cheong)

Chinese sausages can be made up of a range of meats, from diced pork to duck or turkey livers. Different types include *lap chang*, which is a solid, dried sausage made from pork and has a smoky, sweet taste.

Choi sum

This Chinese flowering cabbage is a member of the mustard family. With dark green leaves and a flavour midway between spinach and cabbage, this vegetable is one of the most popular in Chinese cookery.

Coconut milk

Coconut milk is made from the grated white flesh of the coconut, not the liquid found inside the fruit. Smooth and creamy, it is an essential ingredient in much Southeast Asian cooking. Use it as a base for curries and soups.

Coriander root

In Thailand, every part of the coriander plant is used for cooking. The root is more potent than the leaves, and is often crushed with black pepper and garlic to create one of the most widely used basic seasonings.

Dark soy sauce

Dark soy sauce, or *tamari*, is thicker and darker than regular soy sauce. It is made with less wheat and you can also buy gluten-free versions. With its mild and smooth flavour, this seasoning is perfect for more delicate recipes and as a less-salty alternative to soy sauce.

Dashi

Dashi stock can be made at home (see page 156), and is used as the basis for many Japanese dishes, such as miso soup and noodle broth. You can buy several dashi products, including liquid instant dashi, dashi powders and granules.

Dried anchovies

Dried anchovies, or *myeolchi*, are a key ingredient in kimchi. The anchovies are harvested off the southern shores of South Korea and fermented with salt. They are very versatile and can be added to stir-fries and other dishes for some extra crunch.

Dried black mushrooms

These mushrooms are misleadingly named, as they can be brown or even grey, with speckles. Drying gives them a strong flavour and they are great for flavouring stir-fries and soups. They are also valued for their health benefits, as they help to lower blood pressure and cholesterol, and even act as an aphrodisiac.

Dried orange peel

You can buy this in the shops but it is very easy to make at home by drying out scraps of orange peel. Fragrant and zesty, the peel can be ground to make a powder for sprinkling on baked goods or to add flavour to rice.

Dried shrimp

These papery little shrimp have been described as magical because of their ability to liven up any dish. A mere handful is all it takes to flavour a whole pot of soup. Salty and very concentrated, they are dried out in the sun.

Edamame beans

Edamame are young green soya beans, often served as an appetiser in Japanese restaurants. They are commonly eaten straight out of the pod with a little salt but can also be used in dishes such as salads and stir-fries.

Enoki mushrooms

These mushrooms are found worldwide but particularly popular in Japan. They have long slender stems and small caps and a mild slightly sweet flavour. They can be eaten raw and are often used in soups and stir-fries.

Fermented black beans

Fermented black beans, or *douchi*, are made up of dried, salted soya beans occasionally mixed with chilli, wine or ginger. Their dense savoury flavour makes them ideal for enhancing vegetarian dishes and seasoning fish. They are also widely used in China as a base for black bean sauce. Best used in small quantities because of their high salt content.

Fish sauce

Fish sauce is a basic ingredient in Asian cooking. It is usually made of fermented anchovies and has a salty, fishy taste. Use liberally in any savoury dish for an infusion of flavour, or even splash on to cooked food as a condiment. Thai, Japanese and Korean fish sauces all slightly differ in taste according to the balance of ingredients.

Fresh green peppercorns

Green peppercorns are the unripe berries of a tropical vine, and can be used to make black pepper. They have a milder, more complex flavour than black peppercorns, and are said to aid digestion. Buy them fresh on their stems and add them to dishes such as green curry.

Fresh root ginger

This potent root is a staple in South Asian cooking. Hot and fragrant, fresh ginger has a coarse beige skin and can be pink, yellow or white inside, depending on the variety. Grate small amounts into stir-fries or sauces to give some zesty heat, or boil with water to create a soothing tea.

Fresh turmeric root

Fresh turmeric root is often dried and ground into a distinctive orange-yellow powder, popular in Asian cooking. The fresh root is a stark contrast to its dried equivalent. When peeled, the flesh is a vivid orange and releases a fragrant aroma.

Galangal

This root is from the ginger family, but its taste is more peppery than that of ginger and it has a woodier texture. Buy it fresh, dried or ground into powder, and use it in any savoury dish, particularly Thai curries.

Garlic chives

Also known by their Chinese name, *gau choy*, these thick-leaved chives have a subtle garlicky taste. Both leaves and unopened flower buds are used in Chinese cuisine as flavouring in stir-fries, dumplings, broths and other dishes. They are very versatile and similar to chives or garlic.

Garlic roots

These are made up of the taproots of individual garlic plants, and they hold less of a bite than the bulbs. Cook them for a more mellow, nutty taste than garlic, or use raw in dishes like soups and salads.

Glutinous rice

A rice that's grown in Southeast and East Asia, it becomes particularly sticky when cooked.

Gochugaru chilli powder

This Korean red chilli powder is made from ground, dried red chillies and is used widely in Korean cooking. Add a pinch to any savoury dish for heat and flavour.

Gochujang chilli paste

Gochujang, or Korean red chilli paste, is made from fermented chilli, soya beans, salt and rice. It can be very hot and spicy on its own and makes a piquant dip or dressing when mixed with other ingredients.

Green papaya

Green papaya is the unripe fruit before it takse on its rich sweetness and amber hue. At this stage, the skin is green and must be peeled before cooking to reveal its pale, translucent flesh. This flesh is almost flavourless, but can be enhanced with different dressings in Thai salads.

Ho fun noodles

A type of wide rice noodle, ho fun noodles are normally stir-fried with vegetables and meat. Buy these noodles in fresh strips or sheets and slice into strands before cooking.

Hoisin sauce

Strong, dark, salty, and sweet, this Chinese sauce is most commonly used in Cantonese cooking. It's made from a mixture of garlic, vinegar, fermented soya beans, chilli and other varied ingredients.

Holy basil

This popular Thai herb has a sharp, clove-like flavour and is often used in stir-fries. You'll find two types – one with purple stalks and another with green. The purple is more powerful.

Japanese mustard

Japanese mustard, or *karashi*, is made up of ground mustard seeds mixed with vinegar and other spices. It is spicier than British mustard, and you can buy it as a paste or powder. Mix with mayonnaise to create the popular dip, karashi mayonnaise, or use it sparingly as a seasoning.

Japanese sansho pepper

This tangy spice is similar to Sichuan pepper but has more of a lemon flavour. The leaves of the prickly sansho plant are ground and sold as a powder, and it is one of the ingredients in shichimi seasoning.

Japanese Worcestershire sauce

As the name suggests, this sauce is derived from the English sauce of the same name, and is manufactured by the very British-sounding company, 'Bulldog' in Japan. This thick, rich, sweet-savoury sauce is actually closer to brown sauce, and goes fantastically with meat, curries, okonomiyaki and tonkatsu cutlets.

Kaffir lime leaves

These thick, shiny leaves are used in many Thai recipes and can be bought dried or fresh. Tear them to release their distinctive citrusy aroma, and add them whole to curries and other dishes. Try not to eat the leaf itself when served. Fresh leaves can be frozen.

Kimchi

Kimchi is Korea's national dish and South Koreans eat around 40 pounds each of this staple annually. Traditionally, kimchi is made up of pickled vegetables, garlic, chilli, salt and fish. Cabbage is the most common vegetable used. The resulting taste is complex and varies depending on the recipe. The main flavours include spicy, sour and salty, although it can also be sweet if sugar is added.

Kobe beef

Kobe beef is said by many to be the best beef in the world, and is prized for its tenderness, flavour and marbling of fat. Only beef from the *wagyu* breed of cows in Japan can be called 'Kobe' and the animals must be slaughtered in the Kobe region. Stories abound about the cows being fed large amounts of beer!

Kombu

Kombu is made from edible kelp and forms one of the three main ingredients in dashi stock.

Korean anchovy sauce

Anchovy sauce is a crucial ingredient in kimchi. Made up of fermented anchovies, you can use it as a soy or salt substitute in dressings, marinades and soups.

Korean fermented shrimps

Known in Korea as *saeujeot*, these fermented shrimps are widely used in Korean cuisine. Different types are available according to the time of year they are harvested, and they vary in colour and size. Remove the shells before using and add to dips and other dishes.

Korean rice cakes

Also known as *tteok*, these rice cakes are made by steaming glutinous rice flour. There are hundreds of different kinds, both sweet and savoury, eaten at different occasions throughout the year. Common ingredients added include mung beans, red beans, dried fruit, sugar, sesame seeds and oil, and pine nuts.

Krachai

Related to the ginger family, this rhizome is widely grown in Thailand for its spicy aromatic flavour. Its rootlets look like fingers, leading it to be known by the traditional name of 'finger root' in Britain. Cut the root up and add raw to salads and pickles, or cook with soups and curries.

Kuzu starch

This is made from the root of the kuzu plant, which is dried and used for thickening sesame tofu, sauces and other items.

Lemon grass

Lemon grass is a variety of tropical grass with a lemony, sweet aroma. It looks a bit like a fat spring onion, and is a common ingredient in Thai cuisine. The bulb contains the most flavour and can be added whole to dishes or crushed and chopped.

Lotus leaves

These large leaves from the lotus plant are used to wrap food, infusing their contents with their subtle, tea-like flavour. Stuff them with glutinous rice to make traditional Chinese dumplings called *zongzi*, or add other meaty ingredients to fill them.

Lotus root

Also known as *renkon* in Japan, these roots are actually the rhizomes of the lotus *Nelumbo nucifera*. Their sweet, tangy flavour is very versatile, and can be used in a range of dishes. Cut lotus roots into slices to reveal the beautiful lacy structure within. Available fresh, canned or dried.

Mirin

This is a store-cupboard staple in Japanese cooking. A form of sweetened rice wine with a light syrupy consistency, mirin's alcohol content burns off during cooking and leaves behind a sweet taste. Add small amounts to balance savoury dipping sauces like teriyaki, as well as marinades.

Nashi pears

Nashi pears, also known as Asian pears, combine the shape and crunchiness of an apple with the grainy texture and flavour of a pear. They make a refreshing addition to salads and can be used as a sweetener.

Neri-goma

A paste made from sesame seeds, similar to tahini.

Noodles

There's a vast range of noodles in Asian cooking, some made with wheat flour (such as Japanese udon noodles), others with rice flour and yet more with different types of starch such as potato and bean and pea starch (glass noodles). Some noodles are made with egg and they may be fresh or dried.

Nori seaweed

Nori seaweed is most familiar as the wrapping for sushi rolls. It is dark green in colour and made by harvesting seaweed on special farms in Japan. The seaweed is then dried out and pressed into sheets, in a process similar to papermaking. You can buy these sheets in different sizes, or cut them into strips to create a garnish.

Okonomiyake

Okonomiyake are savoury Japanese pancakes, with okonomoyaki flour and sauce as the base ingredients. *Okonomi* translates to 'as you like', and you can add a variety of fillings to the dish according to personal taste.

Oyster sauce

Oyster sauce is thick and brown, with a sweet, earthy flavour. Popular in Vietnamese, Thai and Cantonese cooking, it is traditionally made by simmering oysters in water until the juices caramelise. You can also buy vegetarian versions, made using mushrooms to retain the umami flavour. Add a dash of this tangy sauce to chow mein and wonton noodles.

Pak choi

Pak choi is a Chinese member of the cabbage family, with chunky, pale stalks and dark green leaves. It has a taste somewhere in between cabbage and spinach and has a crispy texture, perfect for salads and stir-fries.

Palm sugar

Not to be confused with coconut sugar, this caramel powder is made from the sap of palm trees. The process of boiling the sap creates a hard, caramel-like substance that can be ground. Coconut sugar is made by a similar process, but using the sap of cut flower buds from the coconut palm. Buying palm sugar can be confusing as it's often packaged as 'coconut palm sugar', so always check the ingredients on the packet to be sure.

Pandan essence

Pandan essence is made by boiling pandan leaves to extract their green colour and nutty aroma. It makes an excellent natural food colourant and is commonly used in desserts and with rice in Thai cuisine.

Pandan leaves

These fragrant leaves are valued in Southeast Asian cooking for their distinctive sweet aroma, similar to that of dried grass. They can be used to wrap savoury food and to lend sweetness and their vibrant green colour to desserts and drinks. Buy fresh or as a prepared paste.

Panko breadcrumbs

These flaky breadcrumbs are lighter and fluffier than the British kind. They are used in most popular Japanese dishes, including katsu curry and as a breading for fried food. When fried, they absorb less oil, making them extra-crunchy and perfect for adding texture to salads and dips.

Pea aubergines

Pea aubergines are small green fruit that form one of the essential ingredients in Thai green curry. They have a slightly bitter flavour, and burst in the mouth when eaten. Add them to curries, soups and stir-fries, or crush them to create tasty relishes.

Pickled ginger

Pickled ginger, or *gari*, is thinly sliced, young ginger that has been marinated in sugar and vinegar. It is usually pink in colour and commonly eaten as a palate cleanser between sushi dishes.

Ponzu sauce

Ponzu is a citrus-based sauce with a thin consistency and dark brown colour. It can be mixed with soy sauce to create seasoned soy sauce.

Rice bran oil

Rice bran oil has an appealing nutty flavour and is often used in Asian cooking for stir-frying and deep-frying. It is made from the inner husk of brown rice and has many health benefits.

Rice vinegar

This mild vinegar is made from rice or sake lees, and ranges from clear to pale yellow in colour. It is an important ingredient in Japanese cooking, with a mellow taste. Traditionally it has been used to preserve food and reduce the strong odour of some fish and meats.

Roasted chilli flakes

These flakes are made up of whole dried red chillies and are very hot. Add them to curries or use them as a condiment in small quantities.

Roasted seaweed

Korean roasted seaweed, or *gim*, is similar to Japanese nori but is often seasoned with sesame oil and salt before it is roasted. It tends to be more delicate than *nori*. You can eat it as a moreish snack or add it to rice and other dishes.

Sake

Sake is Japan's most famous alcoholic drink, made by fermenting polished sake rice. Increasing the amount of rice used and the degree of polishing produces a more refined and aromatic sake. It can be served either hot or cold and, like wine, different sakes go best with different foods. You can also buy cooking sake, which has a lower alcoholic content and can mask the odour of meat and fish.

Seasoned rice vinegar

Seasoned rice vinegar is made up of vinegar, sake, sugar, salt, and sometimes mirin. You will find it in many popular salad dressings, and it is added to rice when making sushi

Seasoned soy sauce

Known as *ponzu shoyu*, this tart sauce is a mixture of citrusy ponzu sauce and soy sauce. Very popular in Japan, it makes a wonderful dipping sauce for sashimi, shabu shabu and other one-pot dishes.

Sesame oil

Sesame oil is one of the most distinctive and fragrant oils you can buy, and is used for everything from dressings to stir-fries in Japanese cooking. Derived from sesame seeds, there are two different varieties – toasted and untoasted. The former is best used as a condiment, sprinkled over dishes at the end of cooking to retain its nutty flavour. Use the untoasted oil for frying and other general cooking purposes.

Shaoxing rice wine

Shaoxing wine is made from fermented rice and is widely used in China as a cooking wine and beverage. It is often added to marinades for meat dishes.

Shichimi (Japanese 7-spice seasoning)

Shichimi is a very popular Japanese condiment made up of seven different spices. The main ingredient is coarsely ground chilli pepper, mixed with ground sansho, roasted orange peel, black and white sesame seeds, hemp seeds, ground ginger and nori. The result is a tasty blend, which can be used to add heat and flavour to noodles, soups and other dishes.

Shimeji mushrooms

Native to East Asia, this group of mushrooms is characterised by their long stems and tight caps. Select mushrooms that are firm and unblemished, and always serve cooked, as they can be very bitter when raw. Their slightly nutty flavour and firm, crunchy texture makes them excellent in stir-fries and noodle dishes.

Shiitake mushrooms

These mushrooms are native to East Asia and are an ingredient in traditional medicines. They are quite mild when raw, but drying them concentrates their flavour. In Japan, they are served in miso soup and are a basis for vegetarian dashi.

Shrimp paste

Shrimp paste is made from fermented shrimp mixed with salt, and can be bought sundried in rectangular blocks or in its wet form. It makes an excellent dip and is an essential ingredient for Thai curries and sauces.

Sichuan peppercorns

Sichuan peppercorns are not actually pepper at all, but the dried berries of a type of prickly ash tree. They are roasted or ground, and form one of the key ingredients of Chinese 5-spice. They have a lemony aroma and famous mouth-numbing quality.

Snake beans

These crunchy beans are long, thin and dark green. They have a slightly sweet flavour and are ideal added to stir-fries and curries. If you can't find snake beans, use French beans instead.

Soya bean paste (or doenjang)

This thick, light brown sauce is a core ingredient in Korean cooking. It is made up of fermented soya beans with added salt, and has a potent, rich taste. Add it to thick soups and stews, or mix with Gochujang chilli paste to create a popular Korean condiment.

Soya bean sprouts

Most bean sprouts you find in supermarkets are made from mung beans, but you can also buy longer, yellow-tipped soya bean sprouts. Nutritious and crunchy, cook them in stir-fries and soups.

Soy sauce

Soy sauce is known for its rich salty flavour. This basic taste has become a foundation of Japanese cuisine, enriching an endless variety of dishes. Soy sauce was first invented in China more than 2,000 years ago and is made by fermenting soya beans in a process that can take years. It is traditionally divided into five main categories based on ingredients and production methods.

Sweetened red beans (azuki beans)

These Japanese red beans are boiled with sugar to form a sweet paste known as anko. Because of their bright red colour they are often cooked for celebrations, and can be used to create a variety of sweet puddings.

Tamarind paste

In Thai cooking, tamarind paste is added to a range of dishes, including pad Thai noodles and *kaeng som* curry. Sold in jars or plastic tubs, this paste is pure tamarind concentrate, and has a very bitter taste. Use with dishes that contain some kind of sweetener to balance them.

Tamarind water

Tamarind fruit has a hard brown shell and green flesh, which turns dark brown as it matures. This pulpy flesh is mixed with water and other ingredients to create tamarind water – a popular seasoning in Thai cuisine. The sweet-sour taste imparts a pleasant tartness to stir-fries, salads and other dishes.

Tenkasu

Tenkasu or *agedama* are crispy pieces of the batter used to make tempura. Small bits come off during the frying process and are removed to prevent burning. Sprinkle them over soups and other dishes to add texture and crunch.

Thai basil

Thai basil is native to Southeast Asia and has a sweet liquorice flavour. Its small narrow leaves are often used in Thai green curry and red curry.

Thai red curry paste

This spicy paste is used to make Thai red curry. Ingredients include aromatic herbs such as lemon grass and galangal, and red chillies. Mix it with coconut milk to create a base for red curry, or add it to stir-fries and soups for a touch of heat.

Thai shallots

Shallots are used in Thai cooking almost as much as garlic. They are smaller and pinker than the European variety, with a strong flavour. Always peel shallots before using. If you can't find Thai shallots use a smaller number of banana shallots.

Tofu

Tofu is made by coagulating soya milk and then pressing it into blocks. It is low in fat and high in protein, making it incredibly healthy. Its bland flavour makes it very adaptable and it readily assumes the flavours of stews, stir-fries and sauces. Buy it firm, soft or 'silken' in texture.

Tonkatsu sauce

Tonkatsu sauce goes brilliantly with pork cutlets to create a dish that is very popular in Japan. It is a thicker version of Japanese Worcestershire sauce.

Udon noodles

Udon are thick, white wheat noodles made from kneading wheat flour, water and salt. You can buy them dried, pre-boiled or fresh. Add them to soups or serve them with a variety of toppings.

Wakame seaweed

Wakame is a thin, dark green seaweed that can be bought either dried or fresh. It is very popular in Asian cooking and lends a sweet, subtle flavour and slippery texture to recipes.

Wasabi paste

This fiery paste has been described as the Japanese answer to horseradish. The wasabi plant is related to watercress and the pale green root is grated to make a powder or paste. The paste is easiest to find, and forms one of the main flavourings of Japanese food. It's seriously hot, so avoid using too much!

Water chestnuts

Water chestnuts are delicately sweet and nutty, with a firm and crunchy texture. Their crisp white flesh can be eaten raw, grilled, boiled or pickled, and they are even ground into flour to make water chestnut cake. Buy them canned or fresh with their distinctive papery brown skin on.

White miso paste

White miso is a fermented paste made from rice, barley and soya beans. It has a slightly sweet taste and is most popular in regions of Japan like Kyoto and Osaka. It is used in miso soup, and also to marinade fish and create filling soup bases for noodle dishes.

Wonton wrappers

Wontons are a type of Chinese dumpling often served in soup or deep-fried. They are made by sealing a small amount of filling, such as minced pork, in a wrapper and then cooking. These doughy wrappers are a square skin of mixed flour, egg, salt and water, and can be sealed by pressing the edges together with your fingers.

Wood ear mushrooms

Also known as cloud ear, these mushrooms are black and twisted when dried, but expand in water, taking on a jelly-like texture. Grown in Western China, they don't have a strong flavour, but instead are enjoyed for their crunchiness. Wood Ears absorb the taste of the dish they are cooked in, and have health benefits including lowering cholesterol.

Yuzu juice

The yuzu is a citrus fruit from East Asia, which looks similar to a small grapefruit. Its light refreshing taste is somewhere between a lemon and a mandarin orange, without being too acidic. In Japan, its aromatic zest is used as a garnish and yuzu juice is a common seasoning that's used much like lemon juice in Britain to add a refreshing tang.

SUPPLIERS

You'll find most of the ingredients for our recipes in supermarkets, but you may need to go a special store or online supplier for some of them. Here are lots of ideas for places to look and we're sorry if we've missed out your favourite. Let us know about it!

ONLINE NATIONWIDE

Hoo Hing
Chinese supermarket network and importer of oriental food and catering products. Next day home delivery service. Stores in Essex, London, Birmingham and Milton Keynes.
www.hoohing.com

Matthew's Foods Scotland Ltd
Scotland's premier Chinese supermarket Branches in Glasgow, Dundee and Aberdeen.
www.matthewsfoods.co.uk

Japan Centre
Excellent range of stock and they deliver all over the UK.
www.japancentre.com

Oriental Mart
Family-run business that started off as an online shopping service. Specialises in Chinese, Korean, Japanese, Thai Malaysian, Taiwanese, Indonesian, Vietnamese and Singaporean cuisine. Delivers to whole of UK and takes requests for items not stocked. Supermarket in Nottingham.
www.orientalmart.co.uk

Oriental Treasure
Family-run Chinese cash & carry supermarket. Sell traditional Far East products. Free delivery for local and national customers. Supermarket in Bradford.
www.orientaltreasure.co.uk

Raan Thai
Europe's largest online selection of fresh, frozen and packaged Thai food and other Asian foodstuffs. Next working day home delivery.
www.raanthai.co.uk

Wai Yee Hong Chinese Supermarket
Family-run cash & carry supermarket offering a wide range of Asian provisions and utensils including Chinese, Thai, Malay, Singaporean, Korean Indonesian, Filipino and Japanese UK next working day delivery.
www.waiyeehong.com

Wing Yip
Established family business, widely recognised as UK's leading supplier of Asian groceries. Located in Birmingham, Manchester, Cricklewood and Croydon.
www.wingyipstore.co.uk

UKCNSHOP
Supplies massive variety of Asian supermarket produce from all over the Far East to both retail customers and businesses. One of the largest online food supermarkets in Europe. Free delivery over £50.
www.ukcnshop.com/en/

SOUTHWEST ENGLAND

Bristol

Wai Yee Hong Chinese Supermarket
www.waiyeehong.com

Dano
206 Cheltenham Road, Bristol BS6 5QU

Oriental Market
13 Gloucester Road, Bishopston, Bristol BS7 8AA

International Food Centre
585–587 Fishponds Road, Fishponds, Bristol BS16 3AA

Exeter

Winmede Chinese Supermarket
Railway Arch, 18 Cowick Street, Exeter EX4 1AJ

Yonk Asian Foods
Summerland Street, Exeter EX1 2AT

SOUTHEAST ENGLAND

Brighton

Fortune Supermarket
Preston Street, Brighton BN1 2HP
www.fortune-supermarket.co.uk

Unithai Oriental Market
10 Church Road, Hove BN3 2FL

Yum Yum Oriental Market
23 Sydney Street, Brighton BN1 4EN

London

Central Oriental
Wide range of products from the Far East and Southeast Asia Supermarkets in Luton, Sandy and Milton Keynes
www.centraloriental.wordpress.com

Korean

Arigato
48–50 Brewer Street, London W1F 9TG

Centre Point Food Store
20 St Giles High Street, Covent Garden, London, WC2H 8LN
www.cpfs.co.uk

H Mart
www.hmart.com

K Mart
kmart-uk.com

Kimchi Village
100 Burlington Road, New Malden KT3 4NT

New Malden Butchers
104 Burlington Road, New Malden KT3 4NT

Korea Foods
www.koreafoods.co.uk

Japanese
Atari-Ya
For top quality sashimi-grade fish
www.atariya.co.uk

Japan Centre
www.japancentre.com

Rice Wine Shop
82 Brewer Street, London W1F 9TG

TK Tradings
www.japan-foods.co.uk

Thai
Hoang-Nam supermarket
186 Mare Street, London E8 3RH

Longdan
www.longdan.co.uk

London Starnight
203–213 Mare Street, London E8 3QE

Chinese
New Loon Moon
9A Gerrard St, London W1D 5PN

See Woo
www.seewoo.com

WALES

Cardiff
Eastern Chinese Supermarket
26–26c Tudor St, Riverside, Cardiff, South Glamorgan, CF11 6AH

The China Supermarket
32–34 Tudor St, Cardiff, South Glamorgan, CF11 6AH

Newport
Eurofoods
Unit E Langland Way, Newport NP19 4PT
www.eurofoods.co.uk

Swansea
Hong Cheong
115 Oxford St, Swansea, West Glamorgan SA1 3JJ

Wah-Yu Chinese Supermarket
145 High St, Swansea, West Glamorgan SA1 1NE

MIDLANDS

Birmingham
Sing Fat Supermarket
334–339 Bradford Street, Digbeth, Birmingham B5 6ES

Wing Yip
www.wingyipstore.co.uk

Leicester
Asiana Leicester Cash and Carry
70 Brazil Street, Leicester LE2 7JX
Online ordering service **www.asianaltd.com**

Tai Fat Chinese Supermarket
5 Melton St, Leicester LE1 3NB

Nottingham
Oriental Mart
www.orientalmart.co.uk

Sheffield
Tai Sun Oriental
17–19 Matilda St, Sheffield, South Yorkshire S1 4QB
www.taisun.co.uk

K H Oriental
Boston St, Off Arley Street, Sheffield S2 4QF
www.khoriental.co.uk

Stoke
Wing Lee
Dennis Viollet Ave, Trentham, Stoke-on-Trent ST4 4TN
www.wing-lee.co.uk

Wolverhampton
East West Oriental Grocery
14 Cleveland Street, Wolverhampton WV1 3HH

NORTHEAST

Doncaster
Tai Sun Oriental Supermarket
49 College Road, Doncaster DN1 3JH
ww2.2.taisun.co.uk

Hull
Chong Wah Chinese Supermarket
8 Union Street, Hull HU2 8HD

Hing Long Hong
59 Spring Bank, Hull HU3 1AG
www.hinglonghong.co.uk

Jing Jing Oriental Food Store
127 Newland Avenue, Hull HU5 2ES

Leeds
Hang Sing Hong
117–119 Vicar Lane, Leeds LS1 6PJ

Newcastle
Wing Hong
55 George St, Newcastle upon Tyne NE4 7JN
www.winghong.co.uk

Brighton Oriental Food Stores
14–18 Brighton Grove, Newcastle upon Tyne NE4 5NR
www.brightonfoodstores.com

7 Days
46 St Andrew's St, City Centre, Newcastle upon Tyne NE1 5SF

Bangkok Minimart
46 Low Friar St, Newcastle upon Tyne, Tyne and Wear NE1 5UE

Scunthorpe
Tradewinds Oriental Shop
29–29A Cole St, Scunthorpe, South Humberside DN15 6QY
www.tradewindsorientalshop.co.uk

Sunderland
Sunderland Oriental Food Store
12A Ford Terrace, Pallion, Sunderland, Tyne and Wear SR4 6LT
http://sunderlandoriental.ueuo.com

York

Oriental Express
8 Matmer House, Hull Road, York
YO10 3JW
http://yorkorientalexpress.webs.com

Fourleaf Oriental Foods
St Sepulchre Gate, Doncaster DN1 1RX

NORTHWEST

Blackpool

Thaitong Thai Supermarket
279 Dickson Road, Blackpool FY1 2JL
www.thaitong.co.uk

Chung Wah Supermarket
40 Cocker Street, Blackpool FY1 2DP
www.chungwah.co.uk

Jade's Far Eastern Food Shop
20 Deansgate, Blackpool FY1 1BN
http://jadesorientalshop.co.uk

Bradford

Oriental Treasure
www.orientaltreasure.co.uk

Fortune Dragon Oriental Food Store
6 Manville Terrace, Bradford BD7 1BA

Carlisle

Chinatown Mini Market
5 London Road, Carlisle, Cumbria CA1 2JU
www.chinatowncarlisle.co.uk

Chester

Spice of Asia
95-97 Brook Street, Chester, Cheshire
CH1 3DX
www.spiceofasiauk.com

Lancaster

Mung Mee Foods
6 Chapel St, Lancaster LA1 1NZ
www.mungmeefoods.co.uk

Liverpool

Hondo Trading Co
Upper Duke St, Liverpool L1 9DU

Manchester

Hang Won Hong
Connaught Building, 58–60 George Street,
Manchester M1 4HF

Kim's Thai Food Store
46 George Street, Manchester M1 4HF

Wing Fat Supermarket
49A Faulkner Street, Manchester M1 4EE
www.wingfat.co.uk

SCOTLAND

Matthew's Foods Scotland Ltd
www.matthewsfoods.co.uk

Aberdeen

The Manchurian
136 Causeway, Aberdeen AB25 3TN

Edinburgh

Orient Thai Market
162-164 Bruntsfield Place, Edinburgh
EH10 4ER

Pat's Chung Ying Chinese Supermarket
199–201 Leith Walk, Edinburgh EH6 8NX
www.patschungying.co.uk

Hing Sing Chinese
310 Leith Walk, Edinburgh EH6 5BU

Huaxing
48 Ratcliffe Terrace, Edinburgh EH9 1ST
www.huaxing.co.uk

Aihua Chinese Supermarket
36 W Crosscauseway, Edinburgh EH8 9JP

Glasgow

Chinatown Groceries
42–66 New City Rd, Glasgow G4 9JT

Seewoo
The Point, 29 Saracen Street, Hamilton Hill,
Glasgow G22 5HT
www.seewoo.com/home

Lim's Chinese Supermarket
63 Cambridge Street, Glasgow G3 6QX

NORTHERN IRELAND

Belfast

Asia Supermarket
189 Ormeau Road, Belfast BT7 1SQ
www.asiamarket.ie

Lee Foods
98–108 Donegall Pass, Belfast BT7 1BX

REPUBLIC OF IRELAND

Dublin

Asia Market
18 Drury Street, Dublin 2
www.asiamarket.ie

Han Sung
22 Great Strand Street, Dublin 1

Oriental Emporium
Unit 1, Rathmines Road, Rathmines, Dublin 6

Asian Food Co.
54–55 Mary St, Dublin 1
www.asianfood.ie

Pinoy Sari-Sari Store
25–26 Little Mary St, Dublin 1; 61 Upper
George Street, Dun Laoghaire, Co. Dublin;
Unit F/G Stadium Business Park, Ballycoolin
Road, Dublin 11
http://pinoysarisari.com

Coreana Supermarket
19 Little Britain St, Dublin 1
www.coreana-online.com

Limerick

Asian Foodstore
2 Gerald Griffin Street Upper, Limerick,
Ireland

INDEX

THANK YOU

To all the lovely people who've joined us on and contributed to our Asian Adventure.

Big thanks to Andrew Hayes-Watkins for some stunning photography and for capturing the mood and the moment in the way that only he can. And to Sammy-Jo Squire for fighting flood, famine, snakes, spiders, heavy seas and wind to get all the ingredients and all the cooking gear to where it needed to be at the alloted time – and for her fantastic help with the recipes and photography. May your super-hero cape never fade.

Grateful thanks to Michele Cranston and Rob Allison for their invaluable advice and input on recipes and ingredients, and their sheer unadulterated passion for food; to creative director Lucie Stericker and our publisher Amanda Harris – as always your support and advice has been a great asset and your love for all things Hairy Biker is a privilege to behold. We love Loulou Clark for her quiet, confident, knowledgeable approach to the look and style of the food and the book – thank you so much, Loulou. And to the magician and wordsmith that is Jinny Johnson, we are eternally grateful for your expertise, knowledge and support in organising our ramblings into what can only be described as a flipping great book. Thanks too to Louis Cunningham Hughes for wonderful assistance at the shoots and to Leah Mitchell for putting together a glossary of ingredients and a list of suppliers – good work, Leah. We love and thank you all.

Special thanks goes to all the very talented shooting crews, directors, producers, researchers, editors and runners involved in filming the Hairy Bikers' Asian Adventure. The list is in alphabetical order, as filming is always a collaborative effort. With much love and gratitude to: Laura Abrahams, Dulcie Arnold, Stuart Bateup, Dan Blackman, Jon Boast, Clare Crossley, Stuart Davies, Katy Fryer, Leanne Hamilton, William Hartley, Mike James, Robbie Johnson, Lucy Kattenhorn, Jungeun Kim, Charmaine Li-Jepson, Jo Lincoln, Mickey Mcknight, Catherine Miller, Chikki Morijiri, Daisy Newton-Dunn, Tim Pitot, Vic Procter, Yoonjung Seo, Matt Smith, Ed St Giles, 'Gong' Pakkawat Supannakran, Holly Wallace, Karen Walsh, Catherine Welton, Deborah Williams.

And we owe a huge debt of thanks to Nicola Ibison, Natalie Zietcer, Tessa Findlay, Rowan Lawton and Eugenie Furniss at James Grant Management for constantly watching our backs, riding shotgun where necessary and shooting from the hip when needed. Without your guidance and input, the Hairy Bikers would have their wheels missing.

Si King & Dave Myers

THE HAIRY DIETERS

EAT FOR LIFE

'Our brand new recipes will help you lose weight & keep it off for good!' Si & Dave x

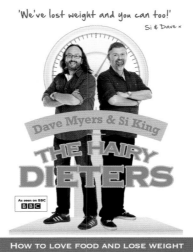

'We've lost weight and you can too!'
Si & Dave x

Dave Myers & Si King

THE HAIRY DIETERS

As seen on BBC

HOW TO LOVE FOOD AND LOSE WEIGHT

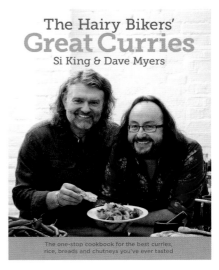

The Hairy Bikers'
Great Curries
Si King & Dave Myers

The one-stop cookbook for the best curries, rice, breads and chutneys you've ever tasted

THE HAIRY BIKERS'
BIG BOOK OF
BAKING

BBC

SI KING & DAVE MYERS

Delicious recipes to take your baking to another level

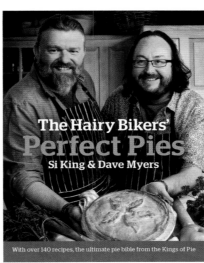

The Hairy Bikers'
Perfect Pies
Si King & Dave Myers

With over 140 recipes, the ultimate pie bible from the Kings of Pie

the HAIRY BIKERS'
BEST-LOVED RECIPES
Mums still know best!
xXx

BBC

Si King & Dave Myers

100 BRAND NEW RECIPES TO COOK WITH LOVE

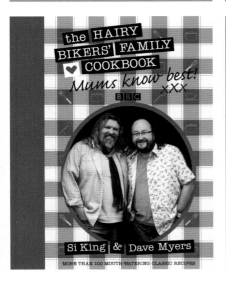

the HAIRY
BIKERS' FAMILY
COOKBOOK
Mums know best!
xXx

BBC

Si King & Dave Myers

MORE THAN 100 MOUTH-WATERING CLASSIC RECIPES

Si King & Dave Myers

the
HAIRY
BIKERS'
12 Days of
Christmas

CHRISTMAS MADE EASY FOR YOUR FAMILY & FRIENDS

FOOD TOUR
The
HAIRY BIKERS'
OF BRITAIN

Delicious regional recipes from the nation's favourite cooking duo and 30 of the UK's top chefs

Si King & Dave Myers

First published in Great Britain in 2014
by Weidenfeld & Nicolson, an imprint of the Orion Publishing Group Ltd
Orion House, 5 Upper St Martin's Lane
London, WC2H 9EA
An Hachette UK Company

10 9 8 7 6 5 4 3 2 1

A CIP catalogue record for this book is available from the British Library.

ISBN: 978 0 297 86735 7

Photographer: Andrew Hayes-Watkins
Food stylist and home economist: Sammy-Jo Squire
Designer and prop stylist: Loulou Clark
Editor: Jinny Johnson
Proofreader: Elise See Tai
Indexer: Elizabeth Wiggans
Photographer's assistant: Kristy Noble
Food stylist's assistant: Louis Cunningham-Hughes
Technical artworker: Andy Bowden

Printed and bound in Germany

The Orion Publishing Group's policy is to use papers that are natural, renewable
and recyclable and made from wood grown in sustainable forests. The logging and
manufacturing processes are expected to conform to environmental regulations of the
country of origin.

www.orionbooks.co.uk